"The problem with communication is the illusion that it has been accomplished".

George Bernard Shaw

"Reading this book, your illusions will be turned to knowledge and you will know that communication has been accomplished"

David JP Phillips

About the author

The human brain, our behaviour and how we perceive and process our surroundings has always fascinated me, to the extent of it becoming one of my true life passions.

Sadly, as a younger man, this passion led me to be known as "the village nerd". Perhaps being the only one of my peers to own their own electroencephalograph brain scanning device didn't help. Personally, I found the experiments I conducted on my friends to be fascinating. But they didn't (not surprisingly) make me very popular with the girls.

Now, fifteen years later, my passion translates into the more preferable epithet of "internationally acclaimed" presenter, trainer and coach within communication and presentation skills. And also author of the book you are holding in your hands - How to Avoid Death By PowerPoint.

For more tips, examples and downloadable templates and files, please join me on:

EN www.thepresentationskills.com
SE: www.presentationsteknik.com

Foreword

Congratulations. You are special! And probably have an above average IQ. The reason being that you have bought and started reading a book which will dramatically increase the efficiency of your communication. Something both you, your colleagues and your clients will benefit greatly from.

However, you are most likely in a hurry, as I often am. Most of us are, but we still need to excel in our daily work. And, like me, you probably seldom have the time or inclination to pick up one of those heavy, 300 page, covers-everything-you-could-possibly-need-to-know-and-a-load-of-other-stuff-you-probably-don't need encyclopedias. And that's why one day I decided to write a series of books, starting with this one, which is the absolute opposite of those.

This book:
- Is condensed to 100 pages
- Includes loads of visual examples
- Only gives you concrete and usable tips
- Always covers every subject in only two pages.
- Is designed to perfectly match the needs of your brain.

If you haven't before, and you start using the principles in this book, your PowerPoint presentations will go from being avoided to being applauded. Better yet, by doing so, your audience will comprehend and remember your messages. Which will lead to less questions and less follow up meetings, thus saving you your most valuable asset in life - Time.

I hope you will enjoy reading this book as much as I have enjoyed writing it. Welcome!

How to avoid Death By PowerPoint
Author: David JP Phillips
Editor: Dave Ferguson
Photographer: Erik Drakenberg

Copyright 2011 David JP Phillips
Printed in Sweden

Published by Presentation Skills Ltd and
the 100 page book publishing company

All images are copyrighted by the author or have
been licensed by the author unless otherwise
noted.M93, David Villarreal Fernández,
SocialIsBetter.

Print History: First Edition, November 2011
Second Edition, September 2015

ISBN: 978-99957-0-111-6

Contents of this book

Presenting with PowerPoint

PowerPoint isn't only about designing and creating slides, very important though that is. An equally and sometimes even more important part is the way your PowerPoint presentation is delivered. Done incorrectly, you can easily send even the most enthusiastic of audiences into a snoozing coma, irrespective of the outstanding brilliance of your slide design. Done correctly, you can gain and maintain high attention and energy levels throughout your presentation.

In this chapter I will deliver to you on a silver platter eight techniques on how to make a great delivery.

Leave the light on

In ancient times, 10 to 20 years ago, the bulbs in video and overhead projectors were so weak that the lights in the room had to be turned off. Today
it is quite different bulb wise, but apparently not people wise. The bulbs
in today's video projectors are great and offer amazing levels of brightness
and contrast. But even though that is the case, in most presentations some
bright spark will automatically stand up and go over to kill or dim the lights.

But maybe our bright spark is a genius after all. What better room than a
darkened one to have a crafty, undetected nap in! Because snoozing is
exactly what turned down or turned off lightning will result in, irrespective
of it being bedtime or meeting time.

So, to start off, leave the light on and keep the room bright.

Avoid bad lightning

Keep the lights on to help keep the
audience bright

Blank the screen

During your presentations with PowerPoint, you may have noticed that the audience focus tend to repeatedly turn back to the screen, even though you are the one talking, trying to convey your message. They're not doing this to be rude. They're doing it because they can't help it. And to know how to handle it we need to understand a little bit more about how our perception works. To illustrate this, close your eyes for a couple of seconds and then open them. You will notice that your eyes involuntarily focus on the brightest areas and objects around you.

This tells us that if you've got your PowerPoint on behind or at the side of you, and it's bright, the eyes and focus of your audience will involuntarily be drawn to your screen and away from you. This is a problem as you are the presentation and the one they should be focusing on. To resolve this, all you have to do is "Blank the screen" with your remote or by pressing the "B" button on your keyboard. Another tip is to always begin your presentation with a blacked out screen so that from the very beginning you become the focal point for the audience.

Keeping a slide on in the background forces the audience to focus on it.

By blanking the screen with the button "B" - the presenter gets all the focus.

Eye contact with the audience

It's late. You're in bed but you can't sleep because you suspect that your partner is out cheating on you. Suddenly, you hear a bang and he stumbles in through the front door. You rush up and confront him! Where have you been?? To hide his cheating he will now either stare right in your eyes or avoid eye contact altogether.

Eyes are often referred to as the mirrors of the soul. We avoid eye contact when we are uncertain, uninterested, scared and even when we tell a lie. These are all triggers and signals that we pick up on in our day to day inter-actions. But when we do the same while presenting with PowerPoint (by looking at the projection screen) we must be aware that we are signalling the exact same things to the audience (uncertainty, lack of interest, dis-trust). I feel safe in assuming that, when planning your presentation, these character traits and signals are not particularly high on your list of ideal audience outcomes.

Your eye contact is of paramount importance and should be focused toward the audience 98% of your presentation time. To make this possible without learning each slide by rote, simply place your laptop in front of you so that you can look down on your slides when you need to instead of looking back and away.

Bad eye contact with the audience.   Good eye contact with the audience.

Use alternative visual aids

Your standard conference room will probably have three types of visual aid at your disposal: the screen for the PowerPoint projection, a white board and a flipchart.

Question - Which one of these three is the most static and unchangeable?

Answer - The PowerPoint presentation.

A static set-up isn't conducive to encouraging audience participation, so be aware that interaction and dialogue will be severely handicapped when using a static visual aid. By contrast, a dynamic visual aid such as the white board or the flip chart will invite conversation, ideas and input from the audience. Personally, I like to have the best of both worlds so I use a Power-Point presentation and a flip chart at the same time.

Use a Flipchart at the same time as PowerPoint.

Project your image on your Whiteboard and draw on it.

Next slide announcement

If you want to become a thoroughbred PowerPoint professional, you've got no other option than to master this principle. The idea is that you prepare the audience for the coming slide, so that they are aware to some extent of the new information. When revealed, they will then be able to process it more efficiently. You do this by introducing its context verbally and then showing the slide.

Quite often the opposite of this happens. The presenter flicks to the next slide, needs a few seconds to understand where he is and what he's going to say, then starts talking. This creates an interruption to the flow and can leave the audience feeling that you are perhaps less prepared or professional than you could be. And if you haven't made the extra effort, why should they take what you're saying seriously?

Like most visual aid programs, PowerPoint allows you to split the screen and get a presenter view on your laptop in front of you. This will show you where you are and which slide will be coming up next. You can then introduce and set the scene for the commencing slide, maintaining the flow of your presentation and keeping the context clear for your audience.

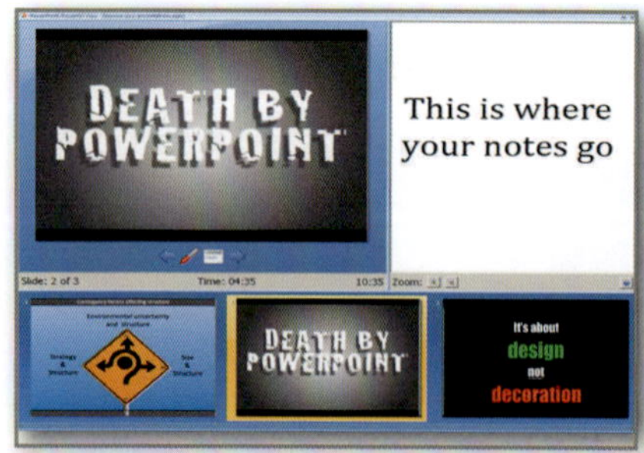

This is the "presenter view" for PowerPoint. It shows current, previous and coming slides and your notes.

Placing the computer in front of you lets you utilize the "presenter view" on your computer.

Use a remote control

When you look at a person, within a split second you can get a sense of how that person is feeling. You can understand a child, even though it can not speak, by observing body language and gestures. Did you know there are seven categories of gestures that assist us to convey our message as presenters? Think how many of these are restricted, or made entirely redundant, when you have to sit or half stand by your laptop.

Your body language informs the majority of the credibility of what you are saying. By confining it you are impeding your ability to convey your message and your presentation as a whole. So my advice to you is: invest a small sum of money in a remote control allowing you to stand, walk around and become as animated as you want. Allow the combinations of thousands of gesticulations to be free! For best functionality get a presentation remote control with 2,4 GHz radio.

A lot of presenter gets stuck by their computer if they don't have a remote control.

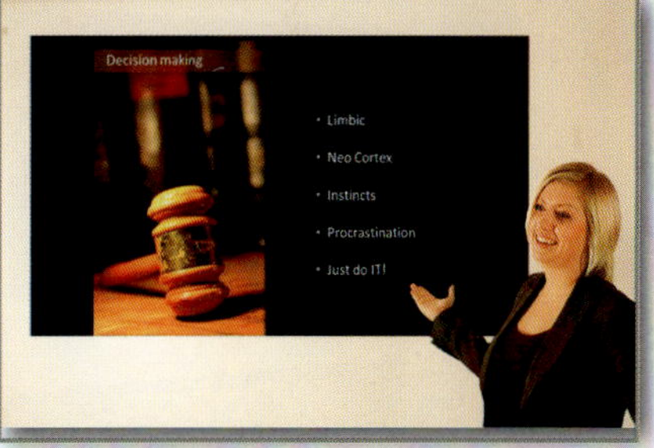

Here we can see a presenter with a remote control which enables her to move more freely.

Avoid using the laser pointer

Just stop for a second and picture a PowerPoint slide so complex and so intricate that you, as a presenter, will need a pointing device with laser precision in order to successfully refer to the right object in your slide! Whatever that slide looks like, somewhere in the design process something clearly very wrong.

And where do you as a presenter end up if you use a laser pointer? Probably to the side of the screen and with your back semi-turned to the audience. A fantastic combination if you are actively intending to alienate your audience. Instead, let go of the laser pointer, design your PowerPoint more clearly and, if you still need a pointer, use yourself, pointing with your hands and arms. Or take a tip from the brilliant presenter Hans Rosling - use a stick of bamboo.

Using a laser pointer forces the presenter to show his back to the audience, resulting in loss of eye contact.

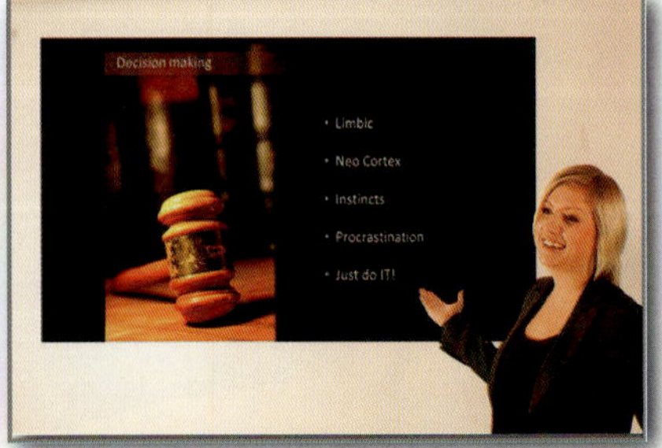

This presenter uses her body language and gestures, enabling her to deliver a much more "live" presentation.

You are the presentation

Somewhere, about three decades ago, PowerPoint was invented and introduced to the masses. Slowly, a misunderstanding started to spread across the presentation world. A revelatory idea had been born. Suddenly, the screen on which we projected the PowerPoint slides on became the presentation! At last, stage frightened managers all over the globe finally had the excuse they had been looking for not to stand in the centre and be the presentation, but instead allow the PowerPoint to be the presentation. How wrong they were.

The undeniable fact is that PowerPoint will never be the presentation. It will always just be a small, accompanying visual aid. You are, always have been, and will for all the foreseeable future be, your presentation. People want to see you. And if you prefer not to see them a good fay forwards would be to attend course in presentation skills or public speaking. Don't hide behind your PowerPoint because your message will never, ever be conveyed as clearly, convincingly and credibly as when you are the presentation.

Don't hide away as a presenter.
The audience wants to be engaged.

You are the presentation, take centre
stage, be the presentation.
PowerPoint will always be
a visual aid. Nothing more.

The 6 commandments

Isn't it amazing - the more we work, the more work we create, which ends up with us having even more work to do! There are obviously several reasons for that catch 22 scenario. I believe that one of the main reasons to it is the way we communicate. A lot of managers I have met tend to dash in to a meeting, deliver their presentation and just leave the result down to hope - "I hope it was a good presentation and that they understood my key message".

The outcome is often the opposite and just generates more questions, meetings and e-mails because people didn't actually understand or remember a lot of the content from the presentation.

So unlike the ten biblical commandments, these six commandments aren't there for your moral guidance, but rather for ensuring that the audience will interpret, understand and remember your content accurately.

And if you are - as the majority of us are - in a mad constant hurry, you will do perfectly fine with only this chapter and these six principles. You can read the rest later when you want to become even greater and take on a little bit more of the world.

1/6 - One message

Keep it simple.
Focus on only one message per slide.

Once in a while you are presented with an aesthetically pleasing slide, but for some unknown reason your brain simply doesn't approve. It's doing its very best, but struggling like mad trying to understand and memorize the new information. The obvious question is: why?

Let's try and think of this another way. Picture a nice Scottish castle with about one hundred billion rooms. All the rooms are connected to each other with about two hundred billion doorways going out of the rooms and one thousand billion doorways going in to the rooms. Can you imagine the sheer size of this castle?

That castle is your brain. The rooms are called neurons and the doorways are called axons and dendrites. Handling this almost impossible amount of neurons and combinations of connections is just amazing, but how often do we just take our brains abilities for granted?

For instance, when presenting a slide to the audience it will take the average brain of some random person a good couple of seconds to figure out which room to store the new information in, to associate that room to other related rooms and to create a memory cue for future use.

The equation here is: The more messages per slide, the longer it will take the brain to process the information and the more likely it will be for the brain to create incorrect memory cues and associations.

So if you want to prioritize the audiences ability to focus, comprehend and maybe even remember your message, it would be a preferable idea to give their brain a break and stick to one message per slide.

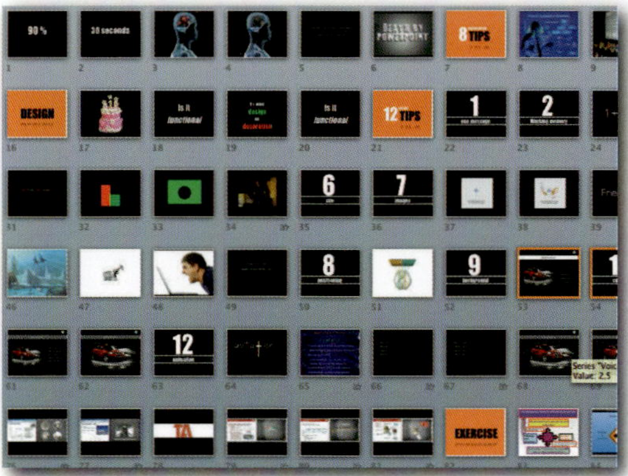

Slide with 2 messages

Two messages per slide is asking for a bit to much from your audience and will quite likely make them shut off instead of turn on and focus on your presentation.

Slide with 1 message

Here we've moved one of the messages (Interior) to another slide, leaving only the one message (engine). The amount of information is now easier for the audience to process.

More slides = better!

By reducing the amount of messages per slide, we obviously increase the total amount of slides. Which is perfectly ok. The problem has never been the amount of slides, the problem has always been the massive amount of messages and objects per slide.

2/6 - Talking and reading

Avoid sentences in your slides while you're talking.

Let's go back in time to a party you were attending a while ago. We find you standing in front of some arbitrary stranger exchanging polite, meaningless conversation about work, interest rates and the latest tabloid gossip. The discussion really isn't going anywhere…

Then, suddenly, you over hear a couple talking about your favourite subject. Your ears prick up and you shift your attention to follow this spark of interest for a couple of seconds, and then come back to your new found mindless-chat buddy. But you now have no clue what the other person is talking about! So you just nod away and answer, yes, yes with polite laughter, desperately hoping that you didn't just agree to something awkward.

You've been there, I've been there. It's an embarrassing moment. And even though our brain is amazing in so many ways, it has no ability what so ever to focus on two conscious things at the exact same time.

John Sweller named this human feature the "redundancy effect" The redundancy effect simply turns the entire use of PowerPoint for the last 30 years upside down. Because it means that if you talk while having readable sentences in your PowerPoint slide, it practically wipes out the working memory, i.e. no long term memory either. This results in it being more luck than anything if, and what, the audience will understand and remember from your presentation.

The crafty quick fix is to let the audience read the slide, black it out and then talk about it. The recommended solution is to reduce each sentence down to a single key word, and then talk about it with the single words as support for both you and the audience.

This is a bad idea!

In this image we can see the speaker presenting while having readable text at the back of her on the slide. This combination is a bad idea if you want the audience to remember your message.

Step 1 - Let them read it

If you have to have a sentence or two in your PowerPoint, a workable compromise is to let the audience quietly read the text for them selves. When you are sure that they are done, you blank the screen as in the example below.

Step 2 - Explain it

Here we can see that the speaker has turned off the PowerPoint slide, thus regaining the audiences attention while explaining the text.

3/6 - Limit your objects

Avoid using more then six objects per slide
Less is more.

Most of you will be familiar with the movie RainMan with Dustin Hoffman. In one particular scene, some matches are dropped on the floor. In less than a split second, "Rain Man" looks down and calculates that there are 246 toothpicks lying there. A truly mind boggling feat.

What's more amazing is when someone gives you a shopping list of, lets say, seven items and you attempt to memorize it. You head off to the grocery store, confident in your ability to successfully achieve such a simple, mundane task. And yet, as sure as the rain falls down and not up, you can clearly remember the first four items, and maybe even the last one, but for the life of you, you can not remember the whole list!

The reason for this is the constraints of the non-autistic-savant human brain. We are all going about our daily business with a severely limited working memory. As a rule, we are only able to hold a maximum of six words (spoken or written) and four images at the same time. This explains why that seventh item is so god damn tricky, and also possibly why convenience stores and corner shops were invented.

What's even more amazing is that, even though we are quite aware of our severely limited working memory, we persist in stuffing our PowerPoint's with such an immense amount of objects that super powers equal to that of "Rain Man" are required in order to fully digest the slide.

So, if you suspect your colleagues lack the necessary autistic abilities, it is advisable that you stay within the limits of their working memory and avoid presenting more than six objects, be they images, words or graphical elements, per slide.

Super Z42 - Engine

A beautiful sleek roadster with six cylinders and boosting a three litre engine with turbo charge gives you the kick you always wanted. Top speeds are reaching close to 300 km/h.

One massive object

A slide with basically two objects. However, one of the objects is so big and contains so much information that it is hard for the brain to get a hold of it - if someone is talking at the same time.

Super Z42 - Engine

- A beautiful sleek roadster
- Six cylinders
- Boosting a three litre engine
- Turbo charge gives you the kick you always wanted.
- Top speeds are reaching close to 300 km/h.

Six objects

In this slide I have reduced the big object above and split it up in to smaller objects, i.e. bullet points. This brings the total amount of objects to six which is a maximum per slide and, sometimes, per group or list.

Super Z42 - Engine

- Sleek roadster
- Six cylinders
- Three litre engine
- Turbo charge
- 300 km/h.

Six perfect objects

In the slide above the bullet points were too long and still caused quite a lot of interference so I have reduced them even further. A good rule of thumb is to keep each bullet point to one context, which usually gives you a maximum of 3 words per point/title.

4/6 - Images

Images outperform words any day

For thousands of years, images, drawings and stories were our primary methods of conveying information. Which may be part of the explanation, why over 50% of our brain is dedicated to visual processes (and also why body language and gesture is such a huge part of communication).

And that is the great advantage of an image - it corresponds to our evolution, a reflection of our only source of information for so long.

And then came words...

When the brain sees a word, what it is actually seeing is an image. In fact, a quite boring image as it's usually just black and white with some lines and curves. It then hastily tries to associate that word with a stored image, which makes the process of transmitting that information a lot easier for the brain. This perhaps explains why storytelling has naturally been the an important source for knowledge transfer throughout the ages.

And then came PowerPoint...

And somewhere, someone got the brilliant idea that even though our brain is optimally wired for processing images, we should solely go over to words.

We know today, through modern understanding of the workings of the brain, that images are superior to words. A single word which is shown to a group will be remembered by about 10%, tested 72 hours after exposure. Showing the same word with an image will increase the performance to 65%. But that's only if the image is black and white. If we show it in colour, we are reaching rates of up to 85%.

It's your choice. Next time you go in to a meeting room, how much do you want your employees, colleagues or audience to remember?

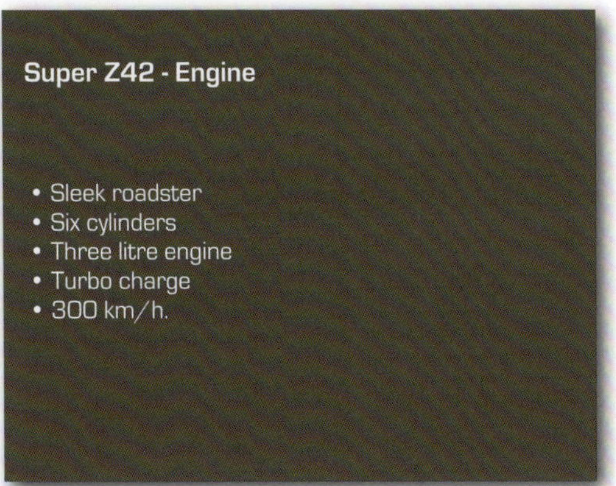

Slide with only text

The slide is clear and easy to read and comprehend. However, as a slide like this lacks emotion and fails to move the audience, it reduces the chances of using emotion to create a lasting memory.

"A picture is worth a thousand words"

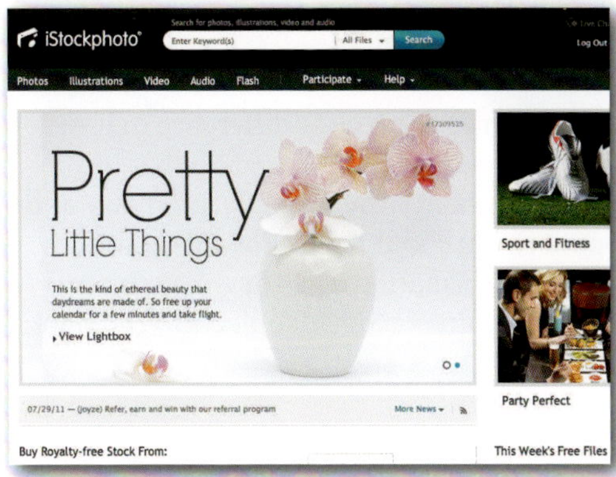

Find great images

There is a huge number of places on the Internet where you can find great images, free and for a fee. So to keep it simple for you, here are my two favourites:

www.istockphoto.com
www.flickr.com

4½ Positioning the image

An image to the left is interpreted with more feelings then an image to the right.

During the beginning of my career, I often noticed that my audience and pupils responded differently to how I positioned the image on my Power-Point slide. This intrigued me and I started making a record of how they perceived an image, depending on if it was presented to the left or the right. Now, ten years on, and nearly 2500 records later, it's clear that there is a definite difference in how we perceive the image showed to us, depending on if it's to the left or the right of the screen.

The reason for this is quite likely to be down to the wiring of the brain. If you look at the first image on the right, you can see that the eyes and brain are cross wired, similar to your entire body. This means that everything you see to the left of your nose is transferred to your right hemisphere, and everything you see to the right of your nose is transferred to the left hemisphere. Now, luckily for you, your two hemispheres are linked through the corpus callosum, so that they can exchange the information. But due to the nature of the hemispheres, they perceive what they initially see differently.

If, for instance, I were to present an image of a speeding car to the left on a PowerPoint slide, the image will be initially processed by the right hemisphere of the person sitting in the audience and it will give that person a sense of movement and speed. This is the opposite feeling you will give the audience by positioning the speeding car to the right of your slide which then will be initially processed by the left hemisphere (i.e. they will perceive less motion in the image).

My conclusion after 2442 records is that there is a clear difference in how an image is perceived depending on its position. And based on that, my recommendation is that if you want to enhance the feeling of an image and encourage a more emotional response, you should place the image to the left. Conversely, if you want analytical information, such as a diagram or a table, to be more easily digested, you should place such objects to the right.

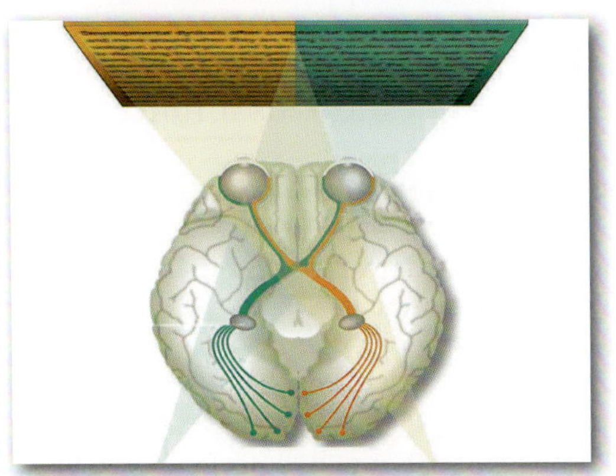

Right vs left hemisphere

In this image, you and your brain see the image of the car and the road to the left and the chart to the right, thus placing them in the opposite regions of the brain and by doing so stimulating and optimizing the perception.

Car placed to the right

Here we can see the car coming in from the right and by doing so being transferred to our left hemisphere, giving a static and emotionless sensation.

Car placed to the left

Here we can see the car coming in from the left and being transferred to our right brain, thus giving a more dynamic, emotional, altogether different sensation.
The image comes to life.

5/6 - Animation

Use discreet animations or animation which emphasise your message. Ask your self the question: "Is it functional".

30 odd years ago, when PowerPoint was first born, some wise guy came up with the brilliant idea of including a couple of dozen animations for a presenter to use. And as time went along, the presenters professionalism and knowledge came to be judged on the sheer amount and variety of animations he had crammed in to his PowerPoint. Extra points could be gained for having matching sounds of typewriters, bombs and speeding cars. Fortunately, this craze passed and, as with all passing crazes, the company behind PowerPoint maybe should have gotten the point that no one really liked the idea of animations. Did they? No. Yet 30 years later, we can now find 5 times the amount of animations in PowerPoint. Absolutely brilliant!

When it comes to animations, you only need ask one question

– "Is it functional?"

Which means that, yes, you can use any of the one hundred included animations, but only if they're functional. If you want an animation flying in from the left, it's okay as long as you work for British Airways. If you want to combine an exploding, swivelling, spouting and zooming animation - be my guest. But let's not forget, this is only appropriate at the annual volcanologists convention.

The most common "YES" answer to the question "is it functional?" is the animation called *appear*. It does nothing but appear, and avoids any kind of disturbance for the audience or create any subconscious thoughts that could distract from the meaning of your animation.

Another usable animation is the *zoom* animation which can visually show something either leaving or coming, which can be quite handy.

Animation no 1

Its always good to start off a slide pretty clean so that you briefly can introduce it and give it the right background. In this slide we have only animated the title, which appears after just showing the image.

Animation no 2 and 3

Here we can see that we have started bringing the bullet points out, two of them to be more precise. As this is a speeding car, we could have got a way with using the animation "fly in" and then prefer-ably from the left as that is "functional" for its design.

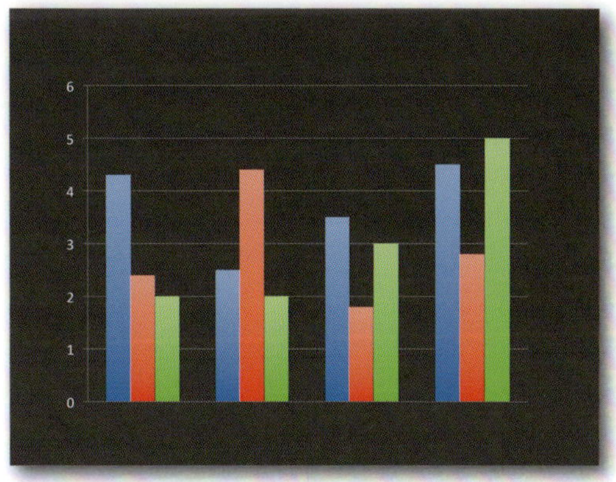

"Wipe" the charts

The animation effect called *wipe* is excellent for charts. It makes them grow upwards giving them the correct "functional' animation. Use *wipe* in conjunction with the set-ting "from bottom to top' to create the best effect.

6/6 - Words or no words

Some words are better to use then no words at all.

As the old saying goes, a picture paints a thousand words. We've known about the impact of a good image for ages. But irrespective of exactly how impressively expressive an image can be, who has the time to spend all day ploughing through Google looking for exactly the right ones? Not many of us. So what's the option? Is it to cut down on slides and only have a few slides emphasizing our message with images, or can I keep the text in my PowerPoint?

And the answer is - keep the text but always minimize it to keywords, no long sentences (at least not while you are talking). Because, even if text is not as efficient as images, it still outperform a solely auditory presentation.

This is referred to as multisensory learning. The renowned Cognitive Psychologist Richard Mayer conducted a study where he split one group in to three smaller groups. The first group received the information only visually. The second received the same information but only auditory, and the third both visually and auditory.

The multisensory group (audio and visual) always outperformed the unisensory groups, showing better instant recall, better long term recall (even after 20 years!) and even better problem solving. The group with the multisensory presentation generated 50% more creative solutions on the first test, and 75% more creative solutions on the second test compared to the unisensory groups. Impressive results.

So the solution to this problem is quite straight forward:
- Keep the words in your presentation but avoid sentences.
- Use images when you want an even greater impact.

Also, remember to use alternate visual aids like a white board or a flip chart to enhance audience interaction and participation.

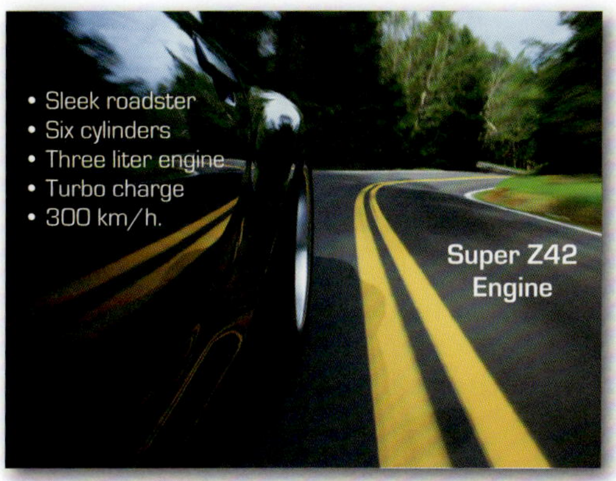

Image with words

An image combined with words gives the greatest of memory impacts.

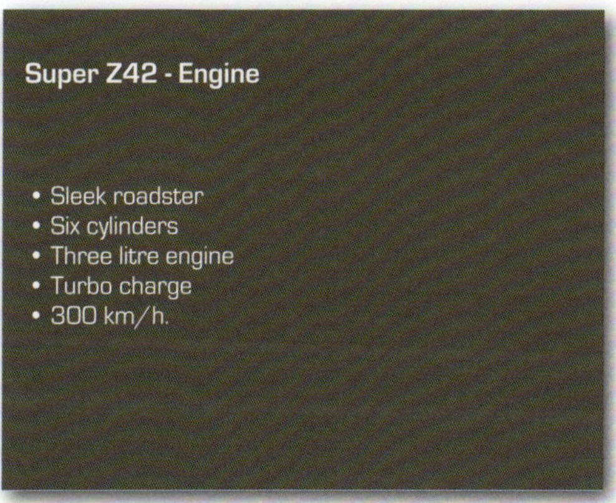

Just words

As you might have noticed, images aren't always that easy to find. When in doubt, just stick with your words in combination with you presenting and talking.

Multisensory

The focus of your presentation is either to make them remember something or act upon something. Multisensory stimulation is the deal. Use it in order to achieve really high impact on all levels.

Magical audience control

We now come to one of my favourite chapters: Involuntary Attention. The reason why it's one of my favourites is that it's as close to magic as it gets.

During this chapter I am going to take you through four basic principles on how to control your audience's attention, without them even realising that you are doing it! We will accomplish this by pushing their instinctive cognitive buttons.

The ability to control your audience's attention has a huge impact as it enables you to ensure that they are homing in like a guided missile on what you want them to be focusing on in your PowerPoint.

1/4 - Colour, Involuntary attention

Red is the fastest colour but be aware of using it as it may not have the same cultural association you want.

Indulge me for a moment. Find a large window and look out of it. Now close your eyes and wait three seconds. Open them again and try to notice what first catches your eye as you take in what's in front of you. It is very likely that you will find that your eyes have involuntarily focussed on objects from a particular part of the colour spectrum. And the most likely colour of these objects is red. Am I right?

In regards to car accidents, it has been shown statistically that red cars are less likely to be involved in accidents compared to cars of any other colour. The reason for this is that red cars will be seen first, because the colour red travels faster then all other colours in the visible spectrum. This is an entirely subconscious response, but nevertheless should maybe be kept in mind next time you are negotiating your insurance premiums.

This is also true for PowerPoint. If you choose to use red to steer the focus of the audience, they will respond because it is the fastest. The speed of colour works according to the visible colour spectrum, as detailed on the adjacent page. Red has the lowest frequency and therefore travels fastest. Violet has the highest frequency and so travels at the slowest speed. There is also an effect called dispersion (angle of the colour).The speed of a colour is almost always constant but in some exceptions it can be influenced by the size of the object and the level of saturation.

It's quite common to use the red to grab the audience's attention. If we utilise this technique, we need to be aware of the genetic and cultural associations that are attached to it. In most western cultures, red symbolises a warning, stop, but also love and passion. So if using red, you must also be aware that the audience will be subconsciously interpreting your choice of colour and attaching emotional responses that are rooted
in their own cultural background. The problem also arises with the use of green. Many cultures associate green with positive responses such as go, ok. Bare this in mind when using these two colours, so that they are interpreted in a way that supports the point you are trying to make, as opposed to causing an obstruction.

Colour Spectra

Colours travel at different speeds according to their position in the visible colour spectrum. Red travels the fastest and violet the slowest.

Fun fact: Green travels fastest in smoke, that's why the majority of exit signs.

Image with red objects

Look at this image, and just feel how your eyes are involuntarily drawn towards the red object.

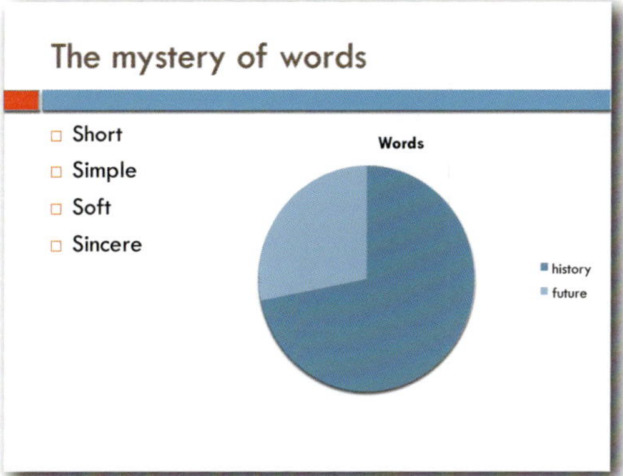

Templates and colours

It's also wise to review your design template. The template should always incorporate "slow colours" in comparison to your content. Otherwise your template, as in the example here with the red detail, will draw attention away from the content.

2/4 - Contrast, Involuntary attention

Use the contrast principle as much as you can in order to steer the focus of the audience.

Using contrast to grab the attention of my audience is one of my absolute favourites. It's very subtle and very effective. Our eyes are involuntarily drawn to areas with high contrast, which means that we can control the audience in a very efficient way.

So what is contrast? Simply put, it is the difference in luminance (light) between two or more surfaces in the same slide or image. The bigger the difference, the stronger the contrast and the quicker it will grab attention. For example, a white object on a black background will generate a 100% contrast and will instantly be the focal point.

There is a simple technique to gauge the level of contrast in your slides. Sit directly in front of your screen and then push your office chair backwards. When you are about a metre away from the screen, perform the infamous squint test. By viewing your slide through your eye lashes, you will see which objects have the greatest contrast. I recommend that you use a chair fitted with wheels. Otherwise, after the "pushing back", you may end up staring at the ceiling, squinting from the sharp pain in your lower back. This will not be helpful.

PowerPoint has actually got a very clever functionality for handling and using contrast to gain attention. What it does is that every time you show a bullet point, it reduces the contrast of the previous one. You will find it by clicking on an animation, and then selecting "effect options". Depending on your version, you will find an option where you can change the colour of the object after each animation. If you then choose a colour with low contrast compared to your background (e.g. grey on a white or black background), it will automatically change the contrast for you during your presentation.

Regardless of PowerPoint's own built in functionality, you should always see to it that the most important object on your slide has the highest contrast. By doing so, you will know where the audience is focusing and that they are focusing on the right thing when you want them to.

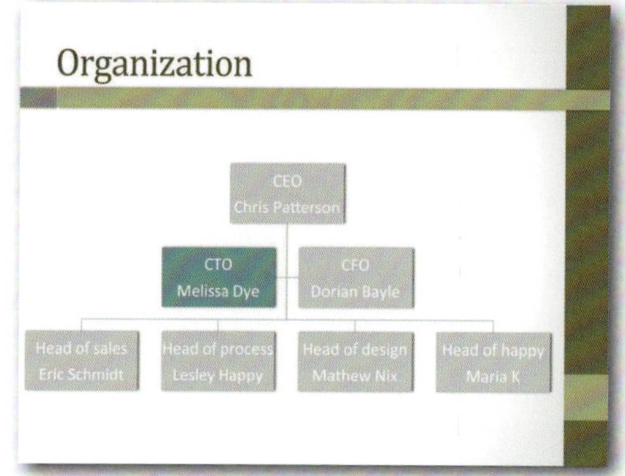

Objects and contrast

In this chart I have reduced the contrast of all boxes bar one, which is left in its original colour. By doing so I am controlling your focus.

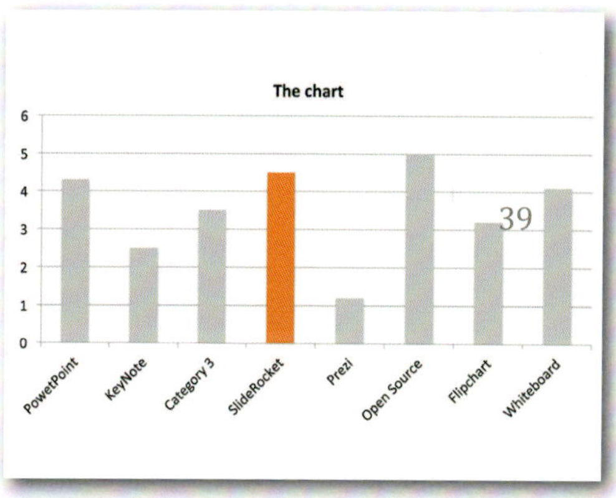

Charts and contrast

Here I have reduced the contrast of the neighbouring bars and left one in its original colour, thus directing your attention to where I want it.

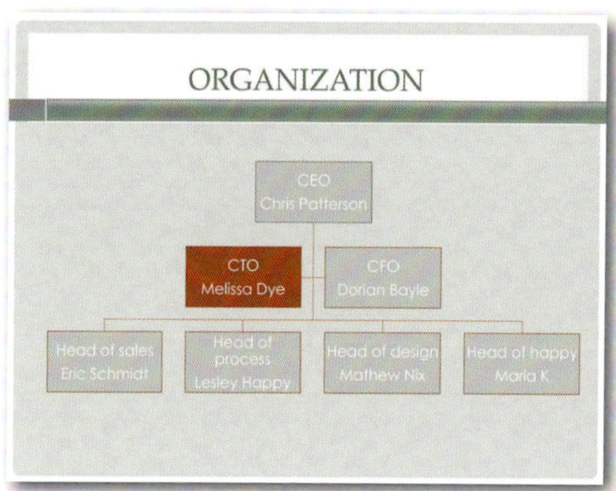

Templates and contrast

Your template layout should have slow colours. The same reasoning applies with contrast. It shouldn't steal focus from the content. In the example we can see how the big white field at the top attracts a bit too much of our attention.

3/4 - Size, Involuntary attention

The largest object is where audience attention will keep returning.

The use, or rather misuse, of size in PowerPoint is one of the biggest mistakes that PowerPoint presenters all over the globe are making. But at the same time, it is one of the easiest things to fix. The reasons for it being such a big mistake is the effect it has on audience attention.

A big object in your PowerPoint will grab the attention of the audience and they will constantly go back to it. This is good, if the largest object is also the most important. If not - then your audience is focusing on the wrong things. Like, for instance, the template. Some templates can incorporate really large elements. This forces the audience to involuntarily look at the template instead of the content of the slide.

Another great mystery is the size of the template titles in PowerPoint. They are constructed in exactly the same way as a word document or newspaper article, where the headline is bigger than the body of text. But in how many cases would you say that your PowerPoint headline is more important than your content? Quite rarely is my guess.

When designing your next PowerPoint, take this into account and try the size principle for yourself. You can test this by running your presentation in "presenter mode", shut your eyes for a couple of seconds and then open them again. You will notice which object your eyes are involuntarily drawn to. Are you sure that you are placing emphasis in the right areas?

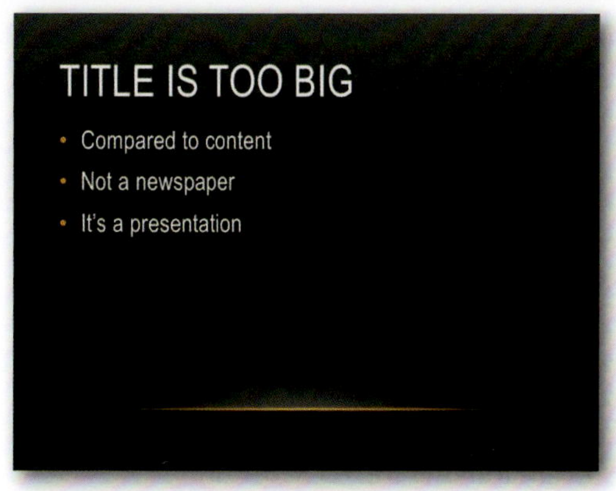

Title is too BIG

In the majority of templates the title is set to be bigger than the content, stealing attention from the most important part of the slide. Here we can see an example of a title on steroids.

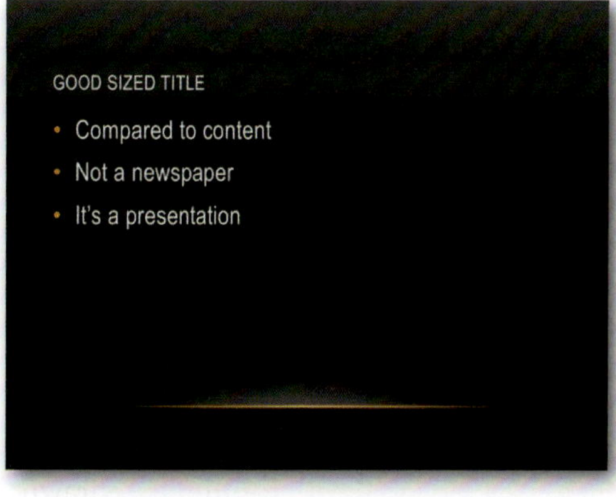

Title is good in size

In this slide I have reduced the title and instead separated it from the content with a low contrast rectangle at the back of the title. The focal point is now more naturally focused toward the content, exactly where I want it.

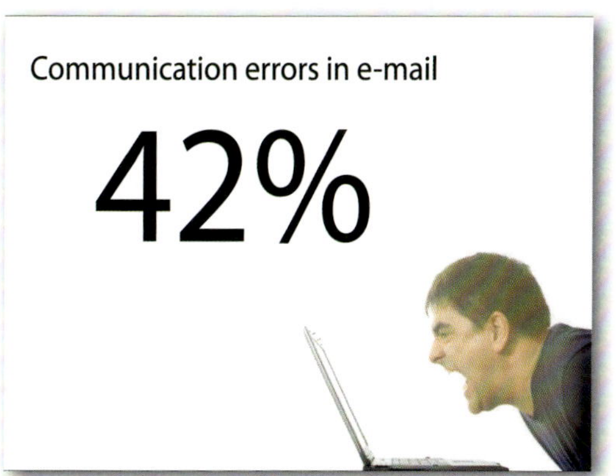

Use of size

This is an example of the use of size, where "42%" is substantially larger then the rest of content and thereby drawing attention to it.

4/4 - Animation, Involuntary attention

Avoid using repetitive animations as an attention grabber.

When surfing the web, standard browsing behaviour on arriving at a page is to have a quick scan and, if we don't find what we're looking for, make for the exit double quick and continue our search elsewhere. The web page owner is well aware that he has a very limited window of opportunity, so he does his damnedest to entice us into focusing on his most important messages. These are often displayed in some form of repetitive animation that is blinking, flashing or moving about and generally being irritating if it doesn't happen to correspond to what you are looking for. As irritating as they are, they are most definitely eye catching and almost impossible to ignore. They have the same effect on our eyes as a light bulb to a moth and become irritating as we find ourselves unable to stop visually bumping into them!

Knowing that repetitive animations are the strongest attention grabbers you can use in a PowerPoint, you should use them wisely. Which basically means almost never. Because, again, the risk you take is that the audience spend too much time focusing on your animation and PowerPoint, and too little time focusing on you and what you are saying.

And this is without even broaching the subject of how phenomenally tacky a repetitive animation can look. I am going to take the bold step of stating that it is not in your best interests to be associated with the annoying feeling that repetitive animations give us while browsing the Internet.

So my recommendation is to avoid using repetitive animations. Only use them when absolutely necessary. Instead, make use of any of the three previous attention grabbing techniques which are a lot more subtle, still highly effective, significantly less irritating, and make you and your presentation look infinitely more professional.

After many hours of tearing out what's left of my hair
and turning idea after idea upside down an inside
out, I finally gave up trying to illustrate and clarify on
paper what a repetitive animation looks like.
So I hope it's clear enough to you without the
visuals for this one.

4

Brain efficient design

Please read and understand this text: USSRYMCAIBMKGB

Don't worry, I know it's annoying - due to the bad brain design of the text above, it can take up to a minute before you figure it out.

Alternatively, what I could have done is used a brain efficient design. In this example, that would mean putting a space in between each of the four abbreviations. This would have made it possible for you to read and comprehend the text in a split second, compared to the several irritated moments it just took you.

And the same thing goes for inefficient brain design in PowerPoint. Done incorrectly, the audience can - as you just did with the sentence above - spend a lot of time just trying to comprehend what your slide actually means.

On the other hand, if your PowerPoint is created with brain efficient design in mind - they can focus all their energy on your message and not waste time trying to figure out what you are rambling on about.

Recognition over recall

Reduce the brain load on the audience by delivering "recognition" instead of "recall"

Have you ever wondered why you feel so exhausted, or, more precisely your brain feels exhausted, when you are travelling abroad? You may be doing more physical exercise walking and exploring than you would normally. But that doesn't really overheat your brain. What does make the brain exhausted are all the new impressions and, more importantly, all the new recalling you have to do: converting currencies, calculating prices, trying to translate the language, relating to different cultural practices and all the other extra bits of work your brain has to do in an unfamiliar environment.

Compare this feeling to when you are at home, in your home town. I would suggest that it would be very rare for you to feel the same kind of exhaustion as when you are abroad. This is because you know everything so well that you just recognize it. To function smoothly, all you need is recognition.

When presenting with PowerPoint, or producing any kind of similar layout, you can decide on either of these two methods. If you want to exhaust the audience's brain - use recall. If you want to them to feel relaxed and at ease - use recognition.

You can easily deliver recognition by using symbolic images, shapes, charts and objects which the audience have seen before and are familiar with. If you use an unfamiliar chart type, they will have to spend time interpreting it (using recall). If, instead, you use a chart type/format that they recognise, then they can focus on the actual message instead of what your chart means.

This is also something important to remember in your own presentation skills, where you should use language adapted to the target group and use examples that they can relate to and easily recognize.

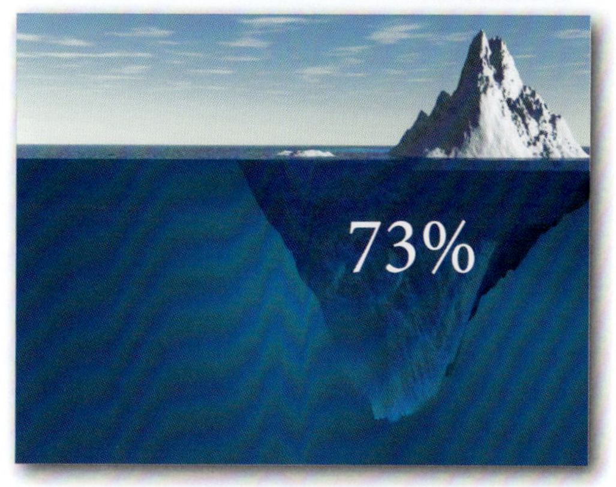

The iceberg

One of the worlds most commonly used symbolic images is the iceberg. A perfect example of recognition as the audience in a fraction of a second under- stands the concept of your slide and your message.

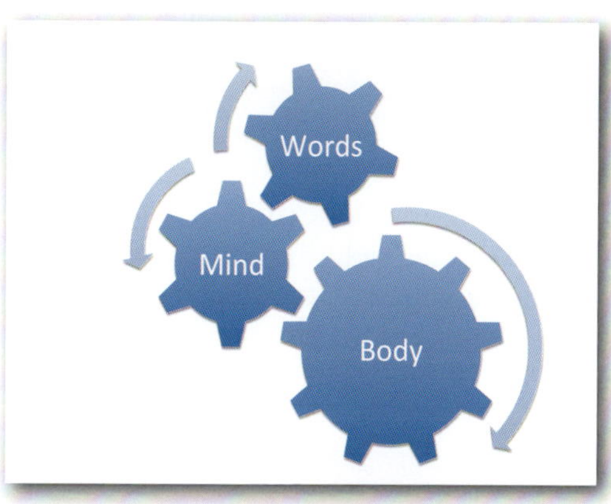

Smart art

In PowerPoint there is a tool called SmartArt which helps you create stunning visual effects like this one. Here we have used classic symbols to show how things are interconnected, giving the slide a good level of recognition.

Weird sign

The last thing you want when coming up to a sign which screams "Achtung!" is confusion. However that's exactly what this sign delivers due to its lack of recogni-tion.

Signal-to-Noise Ratio

Every object, data item and graphic steals attention from the relevant elements in your PowerPoint.

In every presentation you deliver, you are sending a signal. At the same time, you are sending out noise. The more noise you have in your presentation, the harder it is for the audience to pick up on your message and receive a clear signal from you.

It works exactly like a mobile phone and its reception. When you overload your slide with too much information, it's like trying to have a decent conversation in a tunnel on your mobile. No one in their right mind would choose to conduct a serious business conversation when only every other word is comprehendible. But we do tend to do it in PowerPoint, happily filling our slides with too much noise.

So what can we do about it? Minimalism is the way to go here - less is more. Always ask yourself the question "Is it functional?" and if it's not – remove it. In a chart you can quite often remove the grid lines, the chart title and sometimes even the legend. In the actual slide, eight times out of ten you can remove the title, the page number, the copyright text and, if it's an internal presentation, you can even remove the logo (alternatively just have it on the first slide). Be ruthless and remove everything that doesn't lead to your message. Less is more. I know it, you know it, your audience knows it, and they will applaud you for it.

In some circumstances you may want to keep some of the noise, in order to convey the whole message. If that is the case, you can use one of the four methods detailed in the previous chapter to cause Involuntary Attention. By doing this, you will be steering the audience and not letting chance decide what they are focusing on.

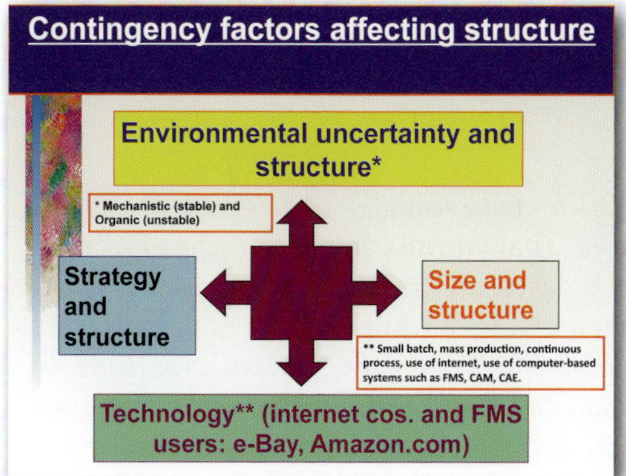

Slide with a lot of noise

This is a noisy slide. Colours, objects, typefaces the lot is making this slide almost unbearable. But trust me, this isn't the worst I've come across.

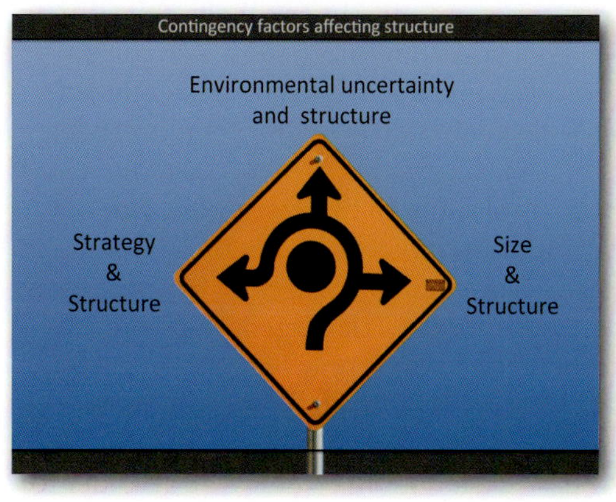

Slide with less noise

This is the same slide as above, or at least it conveys the same message. Some of the rules applied are: Rule of recognition, reduce objects, remove sentences, contrast and size.

Complex information

Use a combination of hand outs and consolidation of complex information.

You've probably been in this situation quite recently: someone is presenting a PowerPoint, and, dutiful employee that you are, you're doing everything you can to stay concentrated and focused on the message. But as time goes by, it becomes increasingly harder and after a while you can literally feel your neurons dying and giving up on you. Then suddenly, without prior permission from yourself, like a lamp switch your brain starts to divert its processing capabilities to nicer, more interesting and, primarily, easier things to busy itself with.

The reason this diversion happens is that the brain can, and will, become overloaded, just like any other processing unit. Put less politely, as well as an overload capacity, your brain also has a boredom threshold that is uncommon in other processing units. However, fear not - there are two excellent ways of saving the day, or rather saving your audience from complex slides:

1. Take your complex information and split it in to two categories. One which you call *presentation* and one which you call *support*. The content that goes into the category "presentation" is what you need to put into your PowerPoint in order to get your message across. The content that you may need to support or clarify your presentation you simply type down in a word document and call it "support". As you commence your presentation, you start off with handing out the word document, which you instruct the audience to read through. When they have done so, you go ahead as usual with your presentation. If needed, you refer to the supporting documentation for more information. Alternatively, you can hand out the support document at the end.

2. Say, for example, you've got 10 slides, all of which are complex. Try to restrict the complex information onto one or two slides, leaving eight easily understood and two highly complex. Before you show each of these two slides, you prepare the audience by saying "This next slide is quite complex so I'll give you a moment to digest it first". You leave it on for 30 seconds or so, so that they get time to view it properly. Then you go ahead and explain parts or all of it, with the help of the contrast principle.

Use contrast

Using the contrast principle is a great way of presenting complex information. In this example you can see lines of code where of one the lines is a lot clearer due to its higher contrast. The same principle can be used on any complex slide.

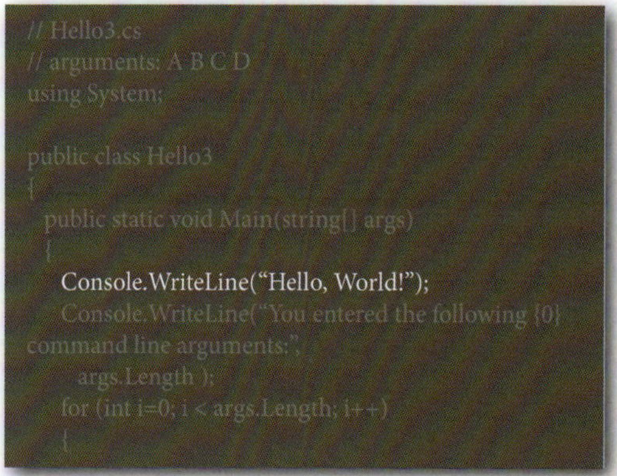

Presentation versus Documentation

There is a big difference between a presentation and a documentation. Respect the difference and avoid presenting documentation to your audience as it is the ultimate sleeping pill.

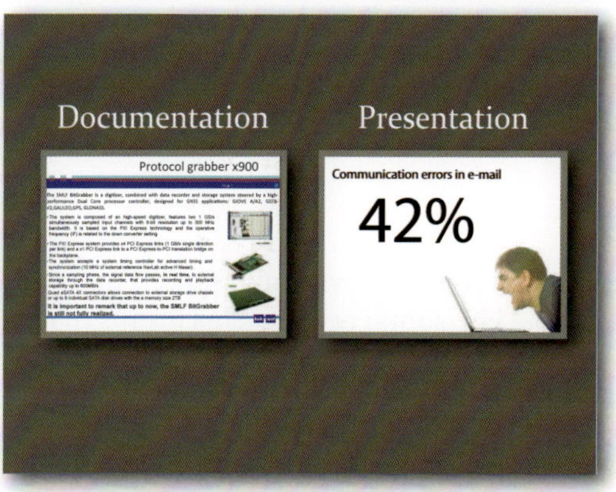

Don't kill your self

Alerting the audience by starting off your entire presentation with saying "This will be a death by PowerPoint presentation" is a bad idea. Because then they know they wont be able to take it, and the risk is that they won't even try.

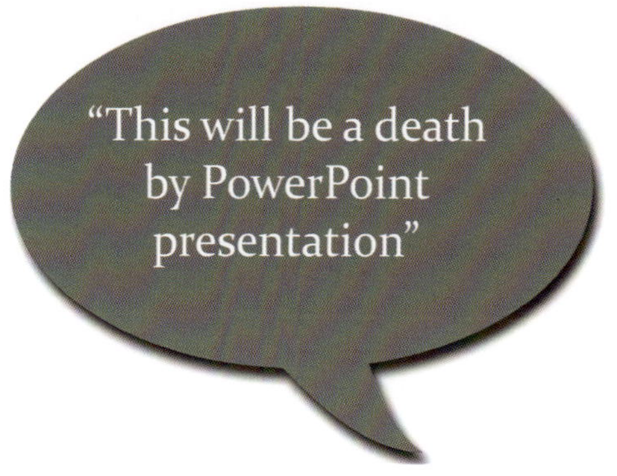

Placement and Purpose

Place your objects accordingly to your purpose. Vertical for prioritization and horizontal for comparing

During your day, thousands of words, images, interactions and other miscellaneous stimuli have informed your choices, mood and decision making. This has happened not necessarily because you wanted it to, but simply because you control only a fraction of everything that your brain picks up and senses in its surrounding. And that is an important parameter to acknowledge when building your presentation - that your audience will interpret its content both subconsciously and consciously. One of the most common mistakes made in PowerPoint is how objects are placed.

Vertical placement

If you have two objects, images or boxes with bullet points and you place them vertically on top of each other, you signal that the one on top is more important, comes first and has highest priority. Which is great, if that is your intention.

Horizontal placement

If you choose to work with the standard template system in PowerPoint, you will notice that your only choice is the horizontal option. This means that two tables, images or text boxes of bullet points are always placed horizontally, side by side. This layout signals a comparison and should be used as such. If, for example, you want to show a comparison between two products and you place them horizontally, that's great. But if you were to place them vertically, you would signal that one is better than the other one.

Both these two layout options are fine, as long as you use them for their correct purpose. And do remember to turn the knowledge around to your advantage. Next time you deliver a presentation to a customer, and you want him or her to choose an option that you prefer, compare two or more products with a vertical layout, thus placing a subconscious thought in the mind of the customer that the first product in the order is the better one. And, as always, the more stimulation the brain (of your customer) gets towards one particular direction, the more plausible it is that they will choose that one in the end. So backing it up with some repetition and good verbal skills will surely result in a win.

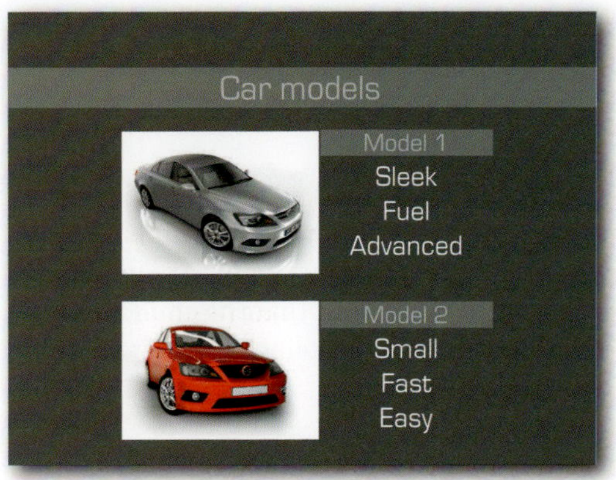

Vertical placement

Placing objects vertically creates a sense of order. Without directly saying so you are intimating that the first option, the option at the top, is the better. A great way of saying something without saying anything!

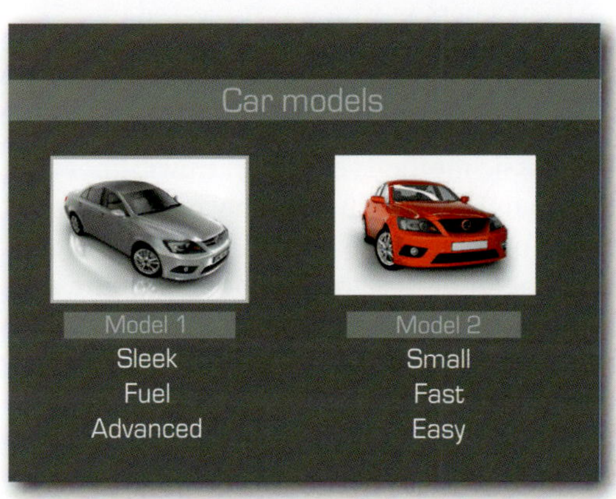

Horizontal placement

Placing objects horizontally creates a sense of comparing and that the objects are equal.

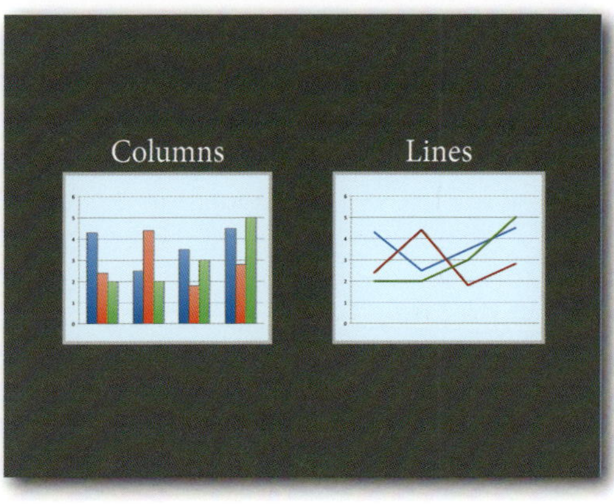

Purpose of the chart

Every chart has its purpose. For optimum recognition use Line-charts for displaying results over time and/ or progression. Use Column-charts for displaying static information such as comparing product sales..

Rule of integration

Make your slide 38% easier to remember by using the principle of integration.

Have you got kids? If you do, or you have kids around you, you may have noticed that they have books - some which you may have bought. Now... did you check for the rule of integration when you bought them? If you did, and the books do apply the principle you can rest assured that the child has a 38% increased chance of remembering the facts. If not, well, let's hope the story in the book is great and looks brilliant.

The number 38% is taken from a study made by Mayer (2005) which showed that a person subjected to a slide with integrated text and graphical elements remembered 38% more than a person who was subjected to separated text and graphical elements. To the right here you can see an example of the two different options.

Apparently, this also excluded the classic methods of using arrows, lines and numbers that we are all too well acquainted with in assembly instructions for wardrobes, chests of drawers and other unfathomable documents. Many of which are most definitely and deliberately designed to induce seizures.

So go through your PowerPoint and see which slides qualify for using the rule of integration and just change things around a bit – in a jiffy your slide will be 38% easier to remember.

Without integration

When the principle of integration isn't applied the text is quite often placed at the side like this:

1. **Beak**
2. **Rump**
3. **Feet**

With integration

Now I have moved the words from the text box and placed them next to the respective objects in the image which means that I have applied the rule of integration.

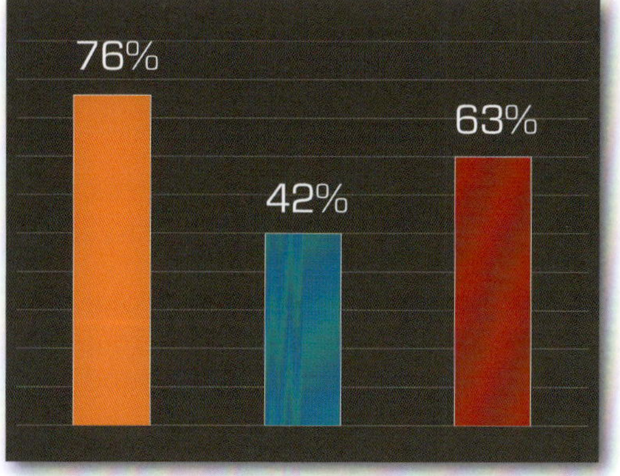

With integration

In this example you can see a column-chart with integrated numbers.

Background

Use a dark or black background for the ease of the audience and the impression of the presenter.

Sometimes I feel that PowerPoint has been severely misunderstood ever since is first birthday. For instance - have you ever asked yourself the question why the background of the majority of PowerPoint presentations is white? It's white! Why? It hasn't always been like that. During the first 10 years, the backgrounds were strangely designed marbled, wooden and semi-psychedelic, spaced out creations. Then someone realized that – hey, that's insane! Let's start using blue and green and backgrounds! Which was a lot better and we stuck to that for about 10 years. And now, for about 10 years or so, we've come up with the similarly mentally challenged idea that we should use white as a background for all presentations.

Great idea. Really? No. Based on these 4 reasons, its a bad idea.

1. When the presenter wants to take centre stage and be the presentation, he can't. Because as soon as he stands in the middle, fronting his presentation, he creates ugly and distracting shadow figures behind him.

2. Having a bright screen behind you as a presenter involuntarily draws all the attention away from you and on to the screen, which isn't what you want.

3. The audience's eyes all have rods (photoreceptor cells in the retina), which are quickly exhausted by the bright light and it eventually induces a headache or tired eyes.

4. When projecting a white background on an otherwise grey screen, you get ugly edges. A dark background, however, melts into the screen, creating a much more aesthetical pleasing impression.

Conclusion: A dark or black background makes life for the presenter and the audience nicer, easier and more efficient. A not so trivial matter.

Please remember that I am referring to presentations with PowerPoint. When using PowerPoint as a report publishing tool, a white background is by far the best. Long sentences need black text on a white background to help reading speed.

White background

A white background is the most inefficient background for a presenter as it steals attention and prevents you from moving due to the shadows that you inadvertently create behind you.

Dark background

A dark background is much better for presenter and audience in several ways.

A beautiful background

A beautiful background isn't always a great idea in PowerPoint as it may divert attention and focus from the content. When picking a background, use a symbolic one for the message and not just the first random great looking graphic you find.

Timelines

Time and progression is and always has been perceived as a horizontal concept.

Picture yourself, twenty thousand years ago. You are sitting around a fire with your tribe, contentedly stroking your belly, dressed in the fur of the giant prehistoric guinea pig that you have just consumed. It's a perfectly ordinary day, maybe even a Wednesday. Later that Wednesday, being an inquisitive sort of Neanderthal, you decide to go exploring and happen to come across your classic dark, damp cave. As you warily enter the cave and your eyes struggle to adjust, a large droplet of icy primordial water splats onto your forehead, sending shivers down your spine. And then, illuminated by a single shaft of sunlight piercing the gloom, you see something. There are markings on the wall in front of you. In the drawing you see a man, no, several men, running after a mammoth in a wild chase for food. You turn your head from left to right, following the flow horizontally as the story develops.

Since that day, twenty thousand years ago, and every single day after that, you and your ancestors have been introduced to the concept of time and progression in a horizontal manner. Your brain has been trained for thousands of years in this concept.

But then out of nowhere...

PowerPoint came along and bullet points changed the illustration of time and progress as we know it. Because now, suddenly, out of nowhere, we challenge the entire history of evolution by presenting time in a vertical manner.

So if you really want to be sure that your audience totally misinterprets your message and gets a particular kind of cognitive misfire, then please feel free to continue with vertical illustrations of progression and time.

But if you want to make it easier for your audience, if you want them to remember the point of your slide - stick to what evolution has done for mine, yours and everyone else's brains, stick to horizontal illustration of progression and time.

A bad example

This timeline challenges evolution as we know it, presenting time and progression in a vertical manner.

A good example

This timeline invites us to clearly understand the concept of progression in a horizontal manner. The text has also been switched to images to further increase retention.

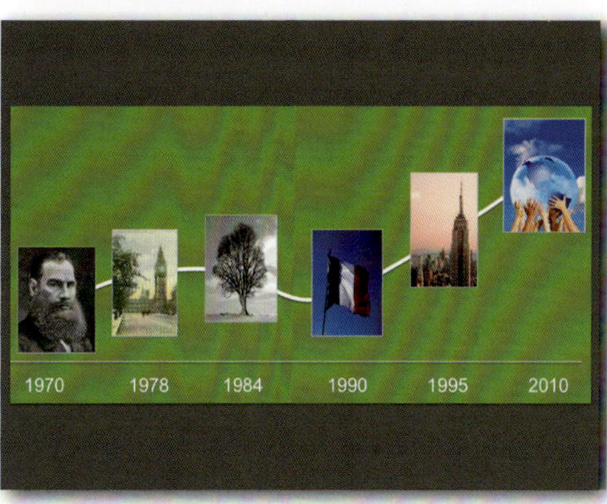

A creative example

Another advantage with horizontal timelines is that you are suddenly able to emphasize the progression by either tilting the time line upwards to show growth or downwards to show decline.

Charts

Stay clear of overly complicated charts and reduce your chart to the least possible elements.

The true killer of cognitive overload for the audience is the chart. Particularly the directly imported and, often, screen captured charts, straight from third party enterprise software. Doing it that way is as clever as sawing of the same branch you're sitting on. A chart is visual and, for its function, brilliant and infinitely better than numbers alone. But as they can easily become too complex there is always a great risk with charts. Which leads us to our main objective on this page - simplification.

Always strive to simplify your chart down to the smallest amount of elements possible. For instance:

- Remove data, bars and lines which are unnecessary
- Use the contrast principle to steer the audience focus in the chart
- Reduce decimals in the axis
- Increase the size of the elements in the axis
- Remove guidelines
- Animate bars and lines
- Remove titles if they're not necessary
- If you only have one data dimension, remove the legend.

In regards to which chart to use, it has been shown in studies by Fischer and Dewulf (2005) that a vertical bar chart is easier and faster to read than a horizontal bar chart. And if possible, try using a pie chart. It is with its one and only dimension the chart which we are able to interpret the fastest.

In general, try to stay clear of more complicated charts. If you aren't absolutely sure that the audience will fully comprehend your latest scatter gun radar chart, it's probably best not to use it.

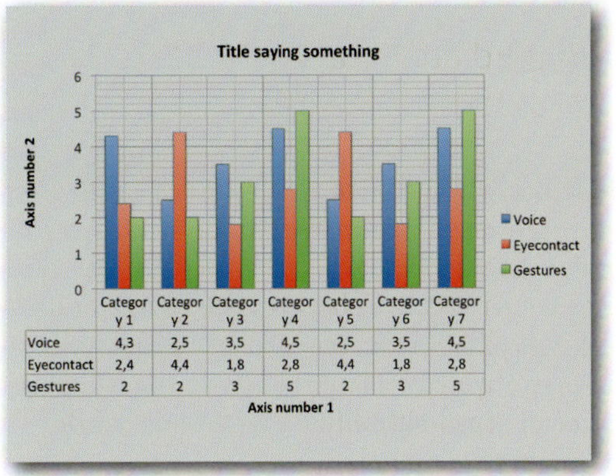

	Categor y 1	Categor y 2	Categor y 3	Categor y 4	Categor y 5	Categor y 6	Categor y 7
Voice	4,3	2,5	3,5	4,5	2,5	3,5	4,5
Eyecontact	2,4	4,4	1,8	2,8	4,4	1,8	2,8
Gestures	2	2	3	5	2	3	5

A massive chart

Here we can see a true nightmare of a chart. Just trying to grasp the basics of what it is trying to convey will take the audience at least a minute. This is fine in documentation, but not in a presentation.

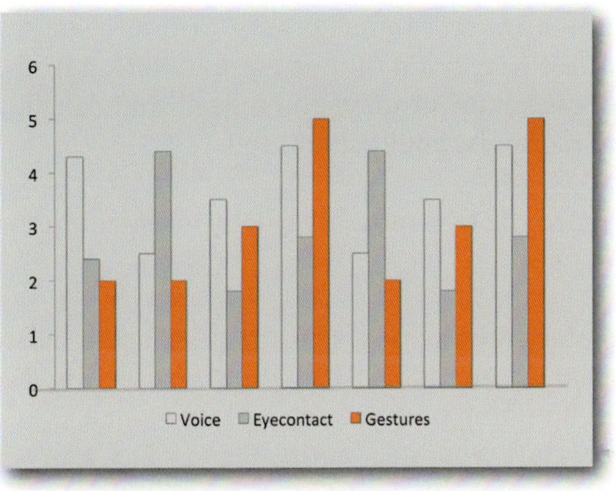

A simplified chart

This is the same chart but simplified. Everything but the absolutely necessary has been removed and the principle of contrast has been applied to bring out the most important data.

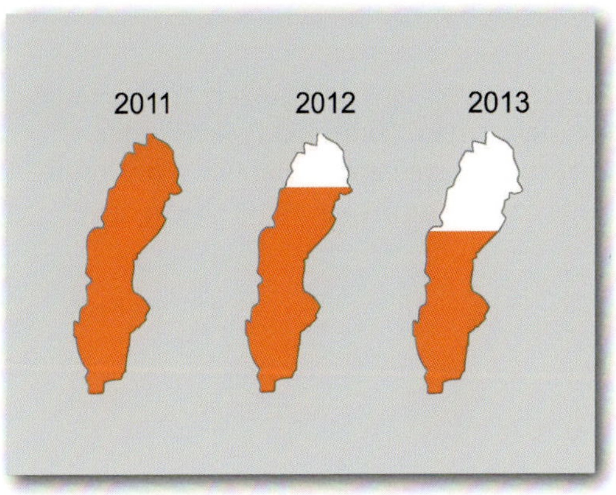

A creative chart

Feel free to use creative charts as these will spice up your presentation. But remember the rule of recognition over recall, and don't go crazy in your design. A good source to learn and get ideas from when it comes to creative charts is the press, the tabloids in particular.

Logotype and templates

Ask your self, is it functional?
If it isn't - remove it.

When poet and playwright Robert Browning coined the phrase "Less is more" back in 1855, he was unwittingly declaring himself to be an expert in the future of communication in PowerPoint.

In the mid-19th century, the workings of the brain were largely a mystery. Today, some 170 years later, thanks to the research of the likes of Mayer and Moreno, we know that memory recall is reduced when extraneous words, images, sounds and graphical elements are included.

And thanks to Slykhuis, Wiebe and Annetta among others, we know that the audience spends a lot of unnecessary brain time attention-shifting from the design elements of a PowerPoint to its actual content. Each shift causing the need for new memories and pathways to be established.

So according to 21st century science, "Less is more" is exactly what it's all about!

But designed PowerPoint templates aren't all bad. The key question is: "Is it functional?" And yes, the logo and the graphical branding are functional in presentations of a selling and branding nature, because that's when you want to really hammer home the corporate identity. But the logo and graphical design elements are counterproductive in other presentations, such as training.

Based on what we know about the brain, you have to be aware that recall and retention will be lower if you stick to using branded PowerPoint's. The solution here is simple - forget the old concept of just using *one* template in PowerPoint and instead have three, as displayed on the right.

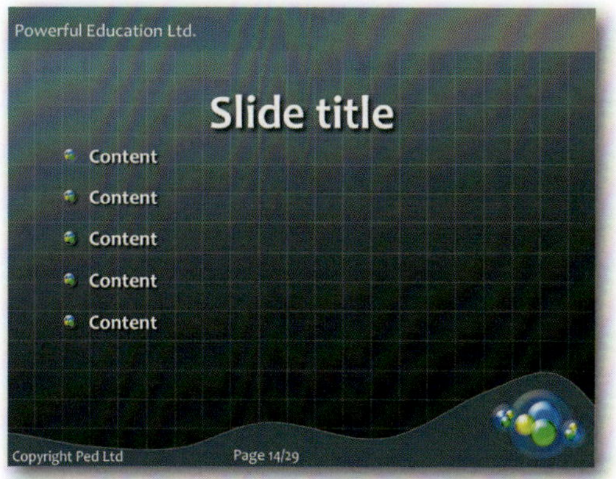

Sales & Marketing template

The template for sales and marketing presentations should have the soul focus of hammering in logo, colours and company name. So a template like this would be OK. However do remember that you place content on second place.

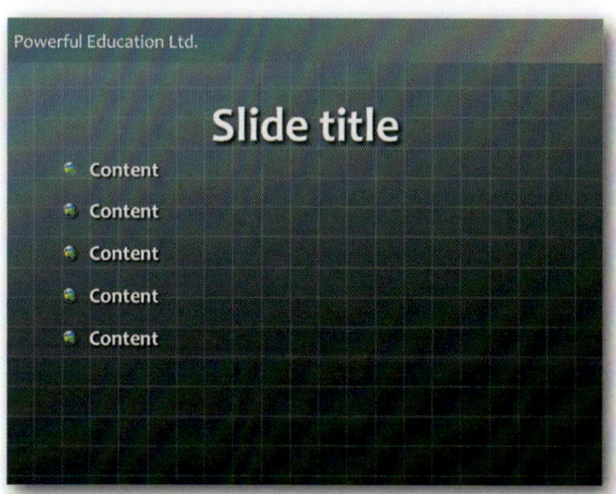

Internal template

For internal presentations, the content is always more important than the branding. So here we have removed a lot of elements and only left colours and the company name at the top.

Template for Training

In courses and other types of training sessions, the content is far more important then the branding. Here we've removed the company name and the branded bullet points and only left the branding colour.

Typeface

The only thing that matters
is the feeling you want to convey.

Let's see, I would like to order a dish of ornamental gaelic roman blackletter. I'll have my BarmenoBQ Medium rare, half a bottle Mistral and my Shruti with a Rockwell Condensed jus. O right, that was the typefaces....

My goodness, how many different variations are there? With tens of thousands of typefaces to choose between, it's far from easy to know which are good and which are not. Which is the best? But there is actually no answer to that question, because it's phrased wrongly.

No typeface is better or worse than any other.

Because the point here is that we're not supposed to use long sentences and massive blocks of text in PowerPoint. That's why there is a different application for that - word processing. When, back in the "old days" (read "now" for the luddites among you), when reams of text were commonplace in PowerPoint, it was beneficial to our audience if we used a serif-font (i.e Times New Roman). Reason being that the serif-font has small feet at the bottom of each letter. Collectively, when put together in a sentence, these feet form an invisible line for the readers eye, increasing the reading speed. But, as we are only supposed to use a few keywords and very rarely a full sentence, the right question is:

So which typeface should I use?

And the answer is: You can use ANY font as long as it supports the message and feeling that you want to convey to the audience. So if you want to be perceived as retro or classic, you should stick to the now 30-year old type- faces such as Times New Roman or Arial. If not, choose which ever typeface you want that supports and emphasises your message. Now on the other hand, don't go wild and include several different typefaces in the same presentation. Stick to the rule "less is more".

Wrong typeface

Combining this typeface with this image is as wrong as it gets.

Matching typeface

Here we can see a better match of image to typeface, conveying a calm, peaceful feeling.

More typefaces

What worries me is that, based on how powerful a typeface is, a corporate template often only allows for one. My advice is to allow more typefaces in order to match the message more effectively, producing a better result.

Formatting text

Increase the reading speed by limiting the line width and avoiding over formatting the text.

As discussed earlier, modern research tells us that using sentences and long tracts of text in a PowerPoint should be avoided. Well, it should be, if it is of interest to you that your audience understand and remember your presentation. So why on earth have I then included a page on formatting text, if you on the other hand are being advised not use sentences?

Well, you can use sentences in your PowerPoint, as long as you are silent while the audience is reading the text to themselves. And this is where the formatting comes in, because an incorrectly formatted text can slow down the total reading speed by as much as 30%. To avoid that happening, and instead increase the reading speed, here are a few things to take into account.

Line width
When we read, we concentrate our eyes on groups of words, often three or four at a time, sometimes less if the words are complicated. For instance, you will focus your eyes 3-4 times per line when reading this text, which is the optimal amount for speed reading 45-60 characters per line. If your lines include more characters, the eye needs to stretch its muscles more, thus reducing the reading speed.

Corrections
When reading text, you may notice that sometimes you have to jump back and read a word or a sentence again. This is called a correction. The more corrections we have to do, the more tired we get, which leads to more corrections, and so on. This will eventually lead to a lack of focus from your audience. The recipe for success here is to minimise the use of long, oddly spelled and complicated words.

Run faster with more feet

In this image we can see what looks like feet on the letters. This increases speed as the eye sees an invisible line. Great to know if you post a quote or longer text in your PowerPoint which you want the audience to read as fast as possible.

Increase reading speed
Avoiding the use of Italic and bold letters are great ways of increasing the reading speed.
The same goes for only capital letters which, according to Miles Tinker (1955), reduces the reading speed by up to 20%.

Twenty years from now you will be more disappointed by the things that you didn't do than by the ones you did do. So throw off the bowlines. Sail away from the safe harbour. Catch the trade winds in your sails. Explore. Dream. Discover.

/ Mark Twain

Call on your partner or colleague and read the text above. Ask them to count the amount of eye fixations you use per line. The lower the number of pauses, the faster you read. The amount of eye fixations is individual and can be trained to increase reading speed.

Go professional

It's autumn and, as tends to happen, there is a chill in the air. So you put on a jacket before walking down to the centre of the town. While walking by a shop window, you notice a finely crafted ornament, which you stop for a second to look at, appreciating the workmanship. Shortly after, a truly beautiful couple pass by. Their features perfectly proportioned, their clothes stylish and well-tailored. You turn around and watch as they walk away. To the right of them, you spot a huge Scarlet Oak, its leaves a sea of deep red, burnt orange and golden yellow. You admire nature's glory for a second or two. But why do you behave like that?

Why do beautiful things draw our attention? It's called aesthetics and the phenomenon can most definitely be used in PowerPoint, in order to make your content and presentation more likeable.

Based on Donald Norman's studies, it has been shown that the viewer/audience will develop a more positive relationship towards the sender if the design is aesthetic, and the opposite if the design is "ugly".

Always aspire to create aesthetic designs as, in every possible way as this will assist you in delivering your presentation and core message. To help you along, here are 6 great techniques to achieve the aesthetic touch.

Consistency

Be consistent, it will make it easier for the audience and allow them to focus on the message instead of the design.

Every breath you take, your brain is interpreting your surroundings, processing over 10 000 instructions a second. But with a limited amount of energy, the brain obviously tries to be as efficient as possible by striving to group things and find patterns. And if it can't find a pattern, it may attempt to try and figure out why. Or it may not bother and just ignore it. Sadly, this is quite a common behaviour of the brain when for a long period of time having to view inconsistent PowerPoint slides. And that is obviously the last thing we want.

Consistency means that you use the same kind of:

- Object
- Shape
- Formatting
- Typeface
- Chart
- Colour
- Images

for the same symbolic value throughout your entire presentation.
You may choose to use two different typefaces in your presentation. But stick to the consistency of using one for the Title and the other one for the Content.

Another example is a chart. Feel free to use different charts, but whenever you show the same kind of information, such as different sales areas and their similar accomplishments, shifting between different types of charts will confuse the audience as it is inconsistent.

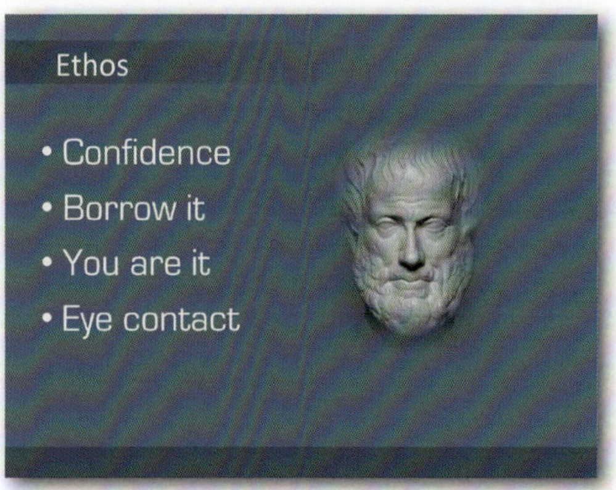

First slide

Here you can see the title being placed in the top left corner and the bullets just below. The image is placed to the right.

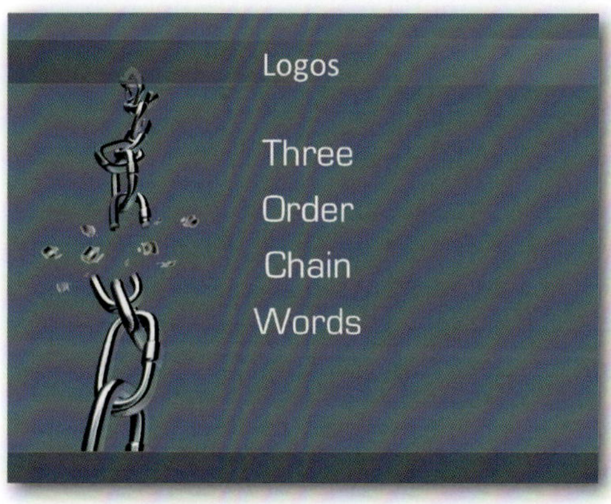

Second slide

In slide number two, the title is now centred and so are the bullet points and for some unknown reason the image has been place to the left. This is an inconsistent layout and will contribute to noise and lack of recognition.

Fun fact

Being seen as inconsistent is a trait which will define the character of that person as being unstructured, unreliable and lacking credibility. The exact same message you will be sending out with an inconsistent presentation.

Alignment

By aligning all your objects you will send out a professional and structured message. Use ALT or CTRL for more control.

A couple of new neighbours have recently moved into your block and have invited you over for a house warming dinner. You come in, sit down on their living room sofa and enjoy a cold beer and some small talk while the food is being prepared. While sipping and chatting away, you notice that behind your host there is a painting on the wall which is about 5 degrees off, tilting slightly to the right. Suddenly you feel the urge to leap up and put it straight. But you barely know these people and don't feel comfortable enough to start rearranging their flat for them just yet. So instead you sit there, festering with your irritation. Then you notice that almost every painting in the house is tilting one way or another. Now you're not only irritated, but you may also start to make judgements about your new neighbours. What's the matter with these people? Can't they see what a state their pictures are in? They must be quite careless and untidy people and, possibly, not very reliable either....

By having objects, shapes, images and texts in PowerPoint that are not aligned, you create similar feelings in your audience. And feelings, as we know, can be both conscious and subconscious. So, whether they realise it or not,you are influencing people's perception of you. For example if you are presenting a new company structure, and everything from charts to labels in your PowerPoint looks like it has been randomly placed, the last thing you are signalling is a good structure.

The eye and the brain love things that are ordered and aligned, and the opposite irritates us. Even down to the smallest fraction of a centimetre.

Have you ever had the problem where you can't really get something perfectly aligned? An easy fix for that is to hold the ALT or CTRL button on your computer (depending on language of the operating system) and then move your object. It will now happily move to exactly where you want it. And if you want even greater precision, zoom in to 200%, and then do the same thing. Poor alignment should now be a thing of the past.

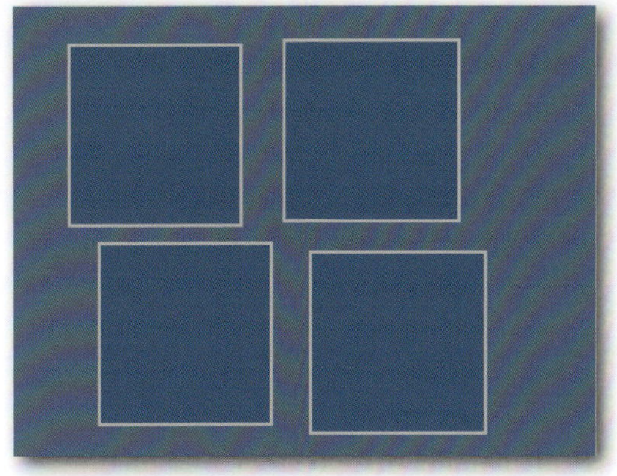

Bad alignment

When working with clients I often come across slides like this one where alignment is off by a million miles. But it doesn't have to be as bad as this to create a negative impact.

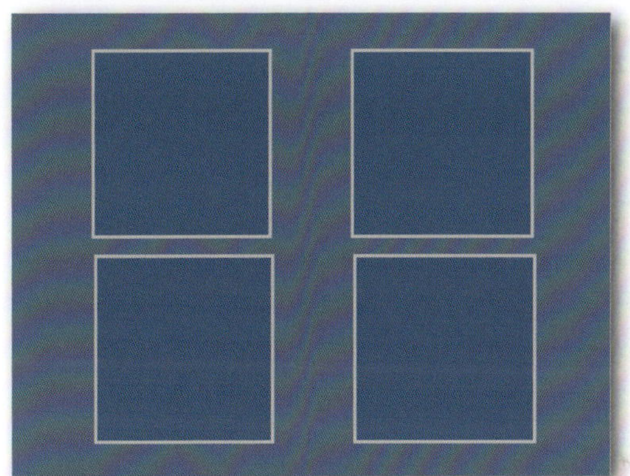

Good alignment

The objects have now been aligned correctly and delivers an entirely different message.

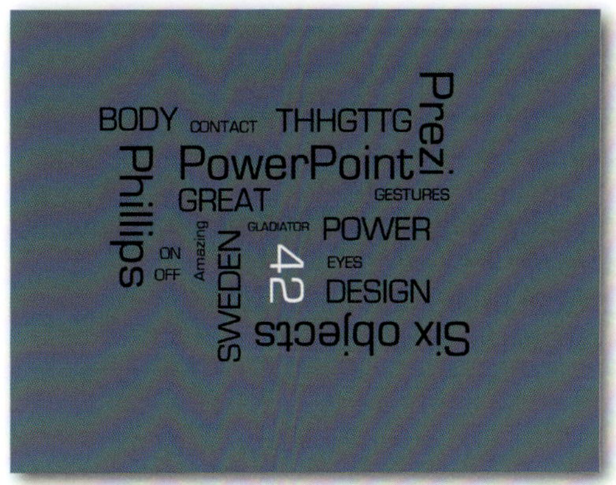

Exception to the rule

And of course, every rule has its exceptions and sometimes there is a symbolic strength in showing several objects which are not aligned, like having loads of words scattered on one slide.

Symmetrical

Keep your layout symmetrical in order to achieve a
professional final result. Use SHIFT for more control.

As with the previous principle of "alignment", we can react negatively to
arrangements in our surroundings which aren't symmetrical.

Picture yourself setting a table for a dinner that is to be a highlight of your
social calendar. You really want to make a good impression and no details
are being left to chance. First of all, in a very considered fashion, you place
the fork to the left and the knife to the right. You are then focused on aligning the knife and fork so that they are parallel to each other. And finally,
you make sure that they are symmetrical, equidistant from the plate. At this
point, it is likely that your child/cat/lumbering partner arrives on the scene
and disrupts your perfect display. They receive the scolding they deserve
and the wandering fork is quickly returned to its original spot in order to
achieve symmetry again.

This urge is strong in us and should be seriously considered when designing your PowerPoint. The audience will, in a similar way to your table-laying
manner, spot your symmetrical discrepancies and, depending on the size of
the disparity, will be influenced in their perception of you and your presentation.

Like the rest of us 150 million PowerPoint users, you've probably noticed
that objects can involuntarily jerk up and down when moving them diago-
nally or vertically. To avoid this, hold the SHIFT-button while moving the
object. It will then move perfectly horizontally or vertically, depending on
what you desire.

The SHIFT button can come to the rescue again if you have inadvertently
made your boss look like they have gained 50 pounds. Keep SHIFT de-
pressed while making an image smaller or bigger and you can be absolutely,
positively sure that the proportions are kept exactly the same as the original.
Phew. Though you may choose to slim things up a bit if you've got a
performance review on the horizon. Never a bad thing.

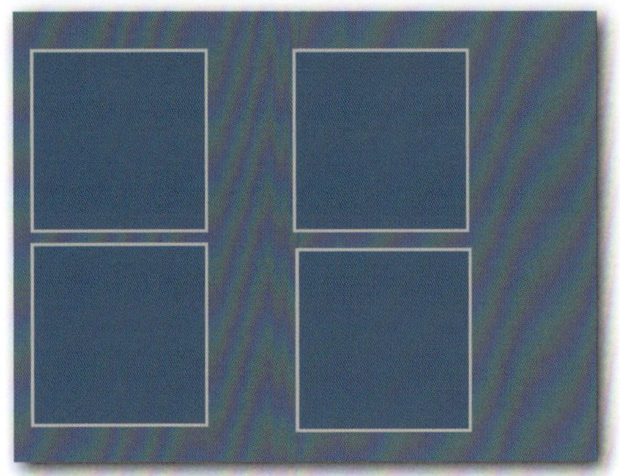

Bad symmetry

Objects which are placed asymmetrically like this shows a lack of professionalism and attention to detail.

Good symmetry

The four objects are now centred and exactly symmetrical when compared to each other and the frame of the image.

Virtruvian Man

Leonardo Da Vinci's Vitruvian Man is often used as a representation of symmetry in the human body and, by extension, the natural universe.

Framing

Frame your objects to create a more aesthetically pleasing and professional design.

In photography and cinematography, framing is a technique used to bring focus to the subject and create a more aesthetically pleasing look.
And I would bet you, that if you had a wander around your home and had a look at the pictures and paintings hanging there, you would find those with well-chosen frames are a lot more pleasant and enjoyable to look at than those that are missing a frame or have been hung with a poorly matched one.

The same aesthetically good, professional feeling can also easily be created in PowerPoint by simply framing your shapes, boxes and images. And in order to do so, you can take one of two paths:

- Choose a colour for the frame which is a complementary colour to the rest of the design.

- Choose a colour which reduces strong contrasts between image and background, making the image more gracefully integrated in the design. This is my favourite! If you go back to the first chapter you can see how I've used it in practice.

As usual, no rules exist without exceptions. The same goes for frames. Certain types of images just look better without a frame, images without a background being one of them.

No frame

Here we can see a slide with an image without a frame.

With a bright frame

In this slide I have used a bright frame to lift out the image from the background making it look more vivid and sharper.

With a dark frame

Here I have switched the white frame for a darker frame which, instead of bringing the painting out, melts it in to the background.

Colours

Impact on the audiences nervous system by selecting the correct colours depending on your intention.

While out driving on a Sunday, you see a sign. At the speed of two hundred million meters per second (that's the speed of light, not the speed of your car), the colours red and yellow hit your retina and are transferred to a brain region called the ventral stream. A split second later, you get the sensation of feeling hungry. What you saw when driving by was the McDonald's logo, or practically any other fast food chain. They all use basically the same combination of colours, all of which has the objective of making us feel hungry.

Red and yellow are not the only colours that can change our mental and emotional state. First of all, it's important to know that colours can affect us from two directions; cultural associations and evolutionary associations. The sheer volume of potential combinations of tone, shade and nuance makes it down right impossible to summarize on one page. So what I give you here are some generic interpretations of the most common colours:

Red - Makes us hungry, alerts us, signals error, danger and passion
Yellow - Makes us alert, awake and happy
Blue - Makes us calm and comfortable
Green - Health, environment, progress and signals good, ok
Brown - Gives the feeling of down to earth, reliable

The second perspective to have in mind when choosing, is to select colours that go well together, that complement each other and that please the eye. My personal method, which gives amazing results, is to use up to four colours taken from images used in my PowerPoint. To find out the names (RGB-codes) of those, we need a colour picker. You can find a colour picker in the expensive Photoshop, the classic tool Paint in Windows and the free tool Splashup (www.splashup.com).

Or if you just want a plain, simple method for picking nice colours, you can look at the "theme-fill-colours" in PowerPoint and only work horizontally with the options available to you. That will keep the saturation at a constant level, which looks good. By switching theme in PowerPoint, you will get a different set up of colours.

Background colours

By using the EyeDropper in PhotoShop I was able to bring out these three colours which I now can use in PowerPoint to create a consistent and aesthetic design.

Background colours

This is another example where I have used the EyeDropper tool, this time from the standard application in Windows called *Paint*.

Theme colours

In PowerPoint you can find the "fill" tool with a basic selection of different colours. By picking your colours either horizontally or vertically you often get a nice homogeneous design.

Transparency

Transparency means that you can make shapes and text boxes see through. By doing this, you are able to let images or backgrounds shine through your chosen shape.

But using transparency isn't a guarantee of success in itself. There is always the risk of creating a bad contrast if you use too much transparency in your shape. As a guide, a good number is usually around 20-30%, but it all depends on the surrounding colours and contrast. So my best advice to you is to try it out, experiment, and just make sure that whatever text you have in your shape or text box is clearly visible. Remember the squint test.

Without transparency   With transparency

Shadows

Using shadows brings a beautiful dimension to a PowerPoint slide, making it look more alive, natural and the word we like - professional. I previously wrote about the importance of being consistent, and the same thing goes for shadows. Select one light source (i.e. that the light source is coming from the top left corner), and see to it that whenever you use shadows in your PowerPoint, they all fall to the right as they would do when the light source comes from top left.

Also, try to restrain yourself from using shadows on letters and words as this tends to look a bit crude and inelegant. Use shadows primarily for images and shapes.

Image without shadow

Image with shadow

Reflections

In the latest versions of PowerPoint it's possible to create a beautiful reflection of an image or shape. The settings for the reflection allow you to play with the size, distance and intensity of the reflection. What's important here is that the reflection looks real and doesn't take over from the actual, all important, content of your slide.

Alternatively, you could also use the effect of the reflection in a symbolic manner, illustrating thoughtfulness and learning from the past.

Almost the same advice goes for reflections as for shadows. Using it on all your text will make a poor impression and lessens the impact. However, using reflections for the limited words in your first, last and/or chapter slides, will look great.

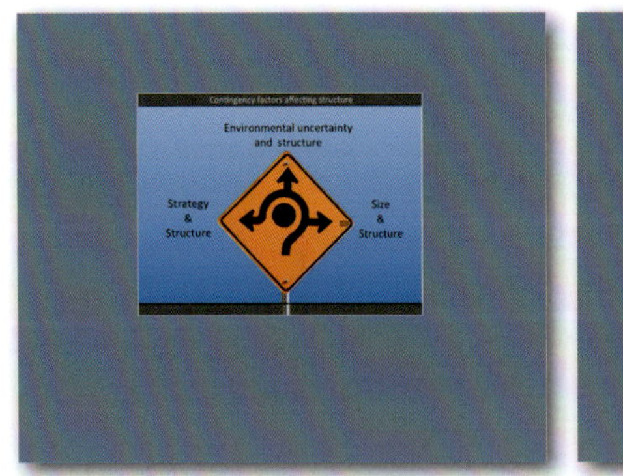

Without reflection

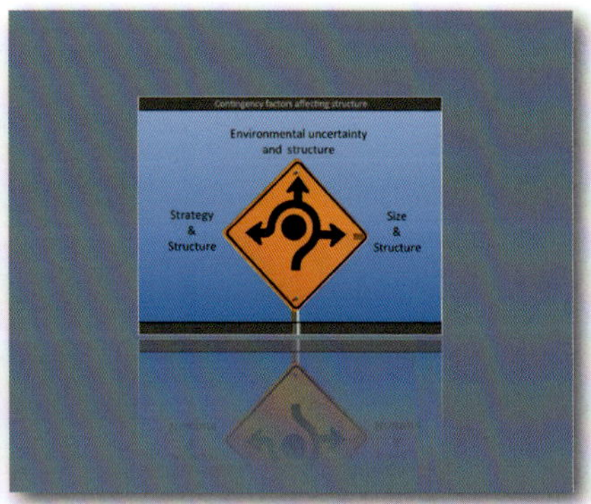

With reflection

Soft edges

Sometimes we find a great looking image on the internet, but it's got this ugly, solid background which makes it look really out of place in our slide. Again, with the latest PowerPoint versions, they have helped us with this by including an effect called soft edges. By using "soft edges" you can remove primarily the edges, but also a lot of the actual background as you can see below.

If you're still stuck with an older version of PowerPoint, you can achieve a similar effect by cropping, which at least lets you remove some of the background. You can then combine the image with a grey frame which reduces the contrast to what's behind it.

Without soft edges

With soft edges

Half time evaluation

1. Well working cooperation between the two organisations in the two countries has led to increased popularity.

2. Participating companies see an effect already in terms of higher turn over, more job opportunities and better development.

3. Emphasise that even if the base consists of thousands of companies, every company is unique and valuable.

1. _______________________________________

2. _______________________________________

3. _______________________________________

4. _______________________________________

5. _______________________________________

6

CHAPTER

Exercise

Well my friend, we are getting towards the end of this book. But before you are tempted to have a look at some further examples, let's see if you - with your newly acquired knowledge and expertise in cognition, psychology and neurology - can do better than the so-called professional PR-firms.

The slide to the left was produced by a Scandinavian PR-firm. They charged 800 Euros for the slide. Let's see if you can do better. Based on what you have learned in this book, can you identify the 5 biggest mistakes they have made? While you're at it - why not pick up a piece of paper and sketch an entirely new version and let your colleague judge your advancement.

And when you're done, let's continue and look at some worked examples.

Examples

Personally, I always love looking at examples. Somehow they seem to inspire me and give me that little extra kick I need to get going and get changing. On the following four pages I have compiled eight examples of Before and After slides from previous client projects for your delectation.

Examples

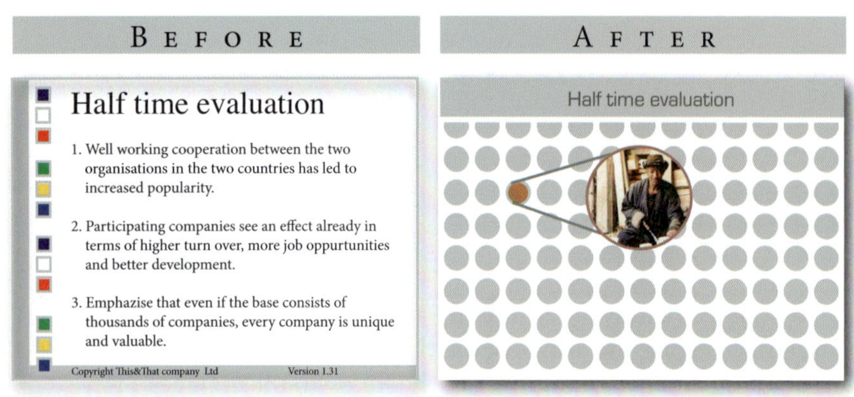

In this example there was way to much information on the slide, so I made three slides of it. The "after" example here represents bullet point number three. And believe it or not, the small coloured rectangles in the original slide are to represent the flag colours of Brazil and United Kingdom. Talk about bad recognition. Who ever paid 800 for that slide should be sacked.

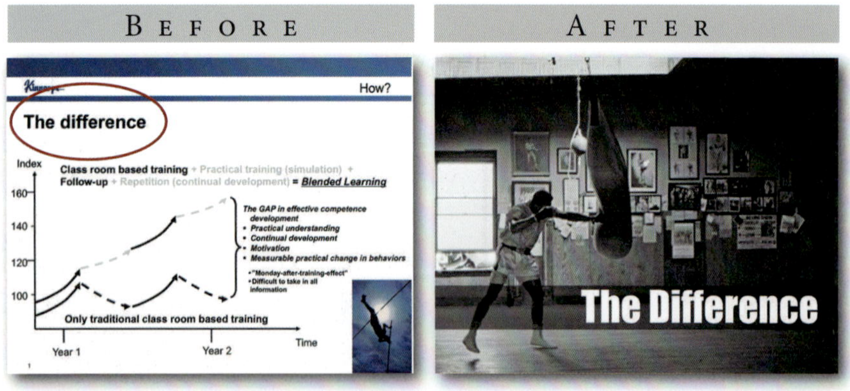

In the majority of slides I've come across, the title of the slide is often redundant and just duplicates the content (i.e. adding noise to the slide). In the example above I have broken out the title to a separate slide and combined it with a powerful and symbolic image.

Examples

<table>
<tr><td align="center"></td><td align="center"></td></tr>
</table>

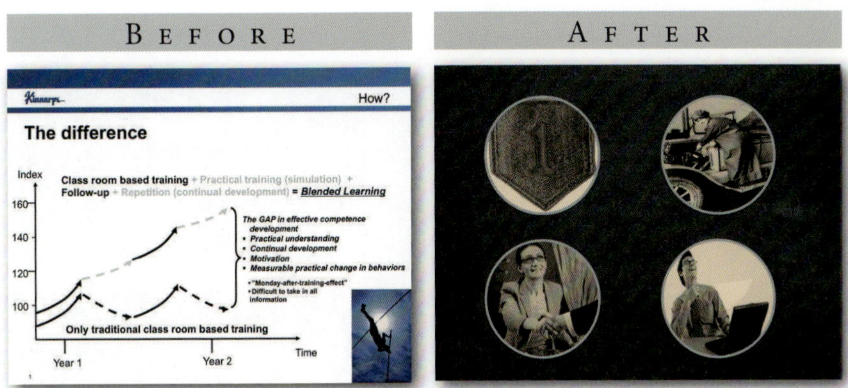

After analysing this slide, we came to the conclusion that the message could easily be explained with four images, each with their own specific symbolic value.

<table>
<tr><td align="center"></td><td align="center"></td></tr>
</table>

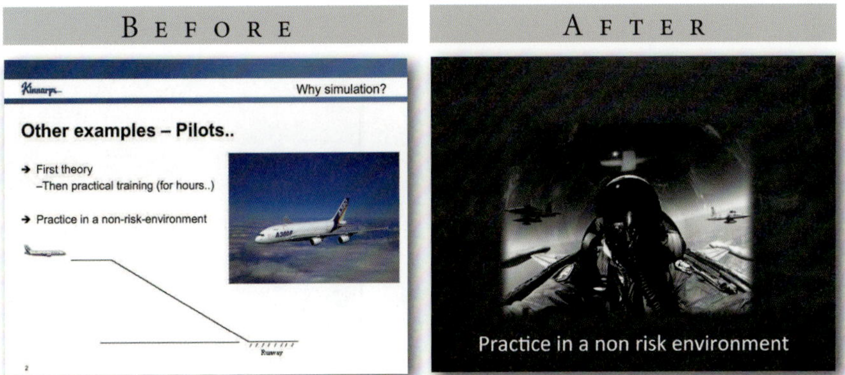

In this example the customer wanted to bring out the feeling and need of serious and real life practice. The sentence is a bit too long, and therefore the presenter was advised to say the sentence before showing the slide and then keep quiet for a moment to allow the audience to digest.

Examples

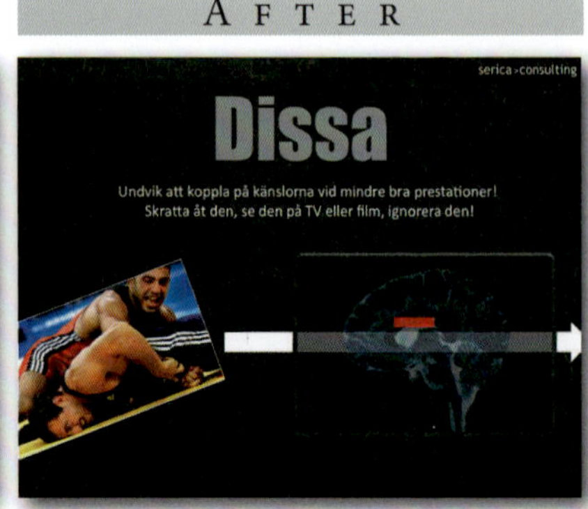

In this example Serica Consulting wanted to lift their entire portfolio of course material to a new standard. I used the principle of size to bring out the most important content, real life images and colour matching for better retention and framing for aesthetics.

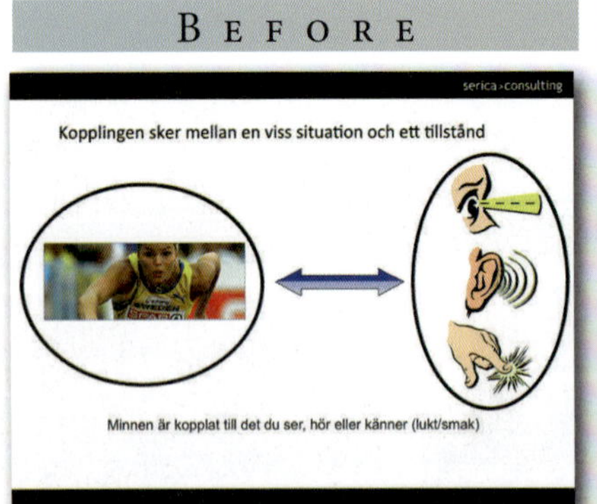

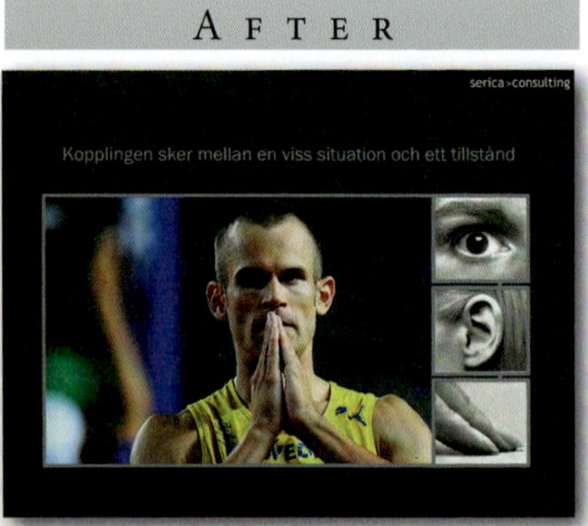

Yet another example where the principle of size, framing, amount of objects and colours has been combined to deliver a clearer slide. The sentence at the top is a little too long, but it's contrast has been reduced in order to reduce the noise created.

Examples

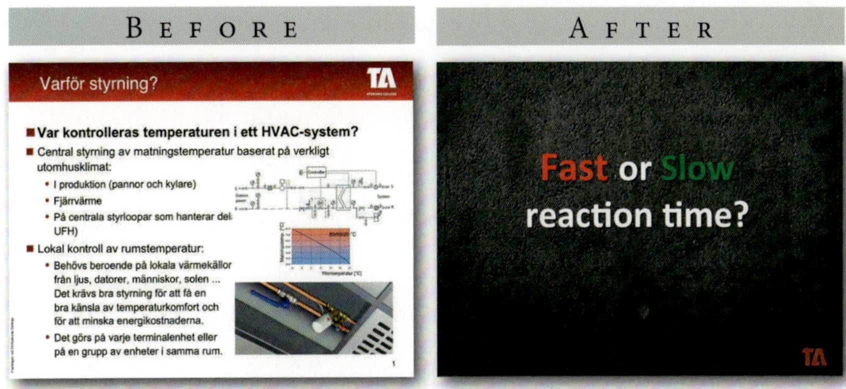

This slide was split into several slides. However, after discussing the content back and forth, we came to the conclusion that the main message didn't have to be more than what is shown in the after slide. The use of contrast, colour and size have been used here.

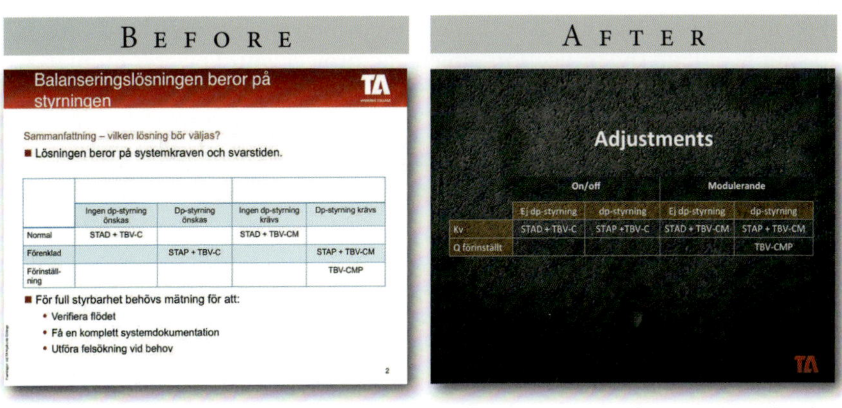

The *Before* table reads:

	Ingen dp-styrning önskas	Dp-styrning önskas	Ingen dp-styrning krävs	Dp-styrning krävs
Normal	STAD + TBV-C		STAD + TBV-CM	
Förenklad		STAP + TBV-C		STAP + TBV-CM
Förinställ-ning				TBV-CMP

The *After* table reads:

	On/off		Modulerande	
	Ej dp-styrning	dp-styrning	Ej dp-styrning	dp-styrning
Kv	STAD + TBV-C	STAP +TBV-C	STAD + TBV-CM	STAP + TBV-CM
Q förinställt				TBV-CMP

Tables are often dreaded in PowerPoint presentations, and sometime they're just not possible to get rid of. What I did here was to clean up the table with consistent colours and remove excess text and the duplication of titles.

Alternate visual aids

PowerPoint is by no measure the only program for visual presentation. Here are a few good alternatives.

Dynamic versus Static
Your first step towards selecting a visual aid is to decide if you want it to be dynamic or static. Looking at PowerPoint and its ilk, they are all very static and tend to make the audience even quieter. The possibility of interaction is limited. So if you want to minimize interaction and dialogue, visual aids such as these are your best option.

However if you do want interaction and dialogue and welcome questions and an engaged contributing audience, you should look at the more dynamic visual aids like flip charts, white boards and post-it's, which can be added to and changed as you go along (i.e. providing opportunities for the audience to interact and feel involved).

The compromise
A compromise between the two options above is to use PowerPoint or Keynote in combination with, for instance, an iPad. That will allow what was a very static format to become dynamic, as you can write and work on the iPad in your presentation. Another option, which is a bit more hard core, is to simply pull up the projection screen and project your PowerPoint presentation directly on the White board. This will allow you to write on the white board at the same time as showing your presentation, getting to use the best from both worlds. A bit like an extremely cheap version of an interactive white board.

Holistical presentations
Microsoft PowerPoint and Apples KeyNote are practically the same thing. They present the content in a linear manner. And so do most of the tools out there, except one ingenious tool called Prezi. Prezi will help you create holistic presentations - perfect for presenting projects, flowcharts and processes.

Prezi

Never before has it been so easy to present flowcharts, processes and other similar holistic information. And as long as you don't zoom in and out too much, it's a great tool even for linear presentations.

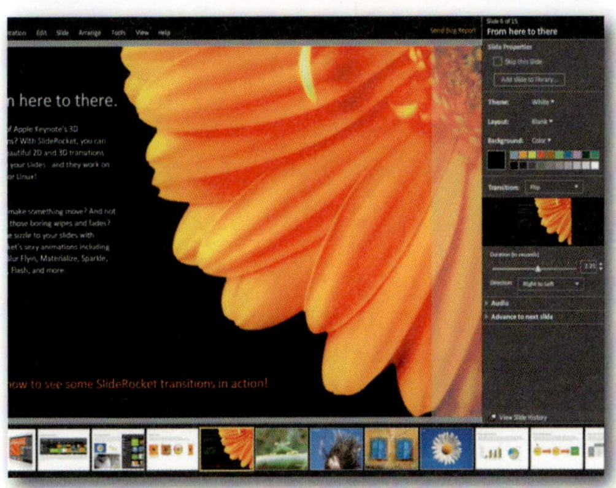

Sliderocket

Sliderocket is more or less PowerPoint on the web and on steroids. Its user friendly, has got almost every functionality you are looking for and, best of all, it is really well integrated with the web in regard to images, videos, quotes and statistics.

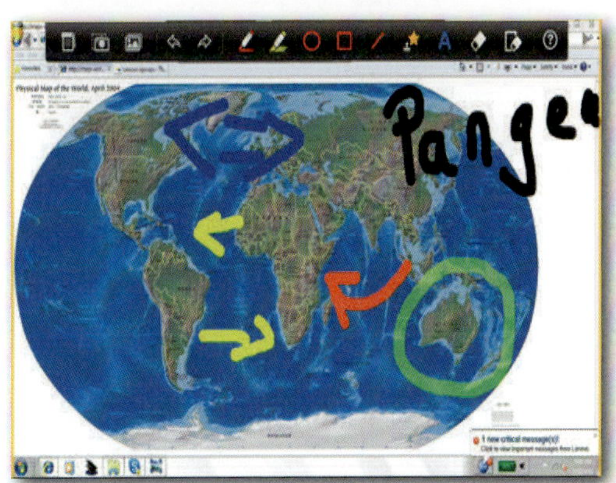

Splashtop whiteboard

If you've got an iPad you're in for a treat with this application. It will allow you to create an interactive whiteboard and annotate on anything that displays on the controlling computer (even flash). You can even save snap- shots and give them to the audience.

Index - Find it here:

Useful resources and inspiration

Great resources to immerse further in the subject

Books

Slide:ology by Nancy Duarte
An extremely comprehensive book on everything you would ever need to know about designing a Visual presentation.

Presentationzen by Garr Reynolds
Garr is a very thoughtfull and warm presenter, and so is his book. An excellent book on the ideas of "less is more".

Brain Rules by John Medina
A brilliant neurology book about the brain which covers the latest and the best information on what we know today.

Websites

TED.com
An amazing site which holds hundreds of full length seminars to be inspired from.

SlideShare.net
For inspiration this website is a must. Millions of Power Point have been uploaded and are yours to be inspired by.

ThePresentationSkills.com / Presentationsteknik.com
My aim is to create the biggest resource in the world for Presentation Skills. You will find extensive articles, tips and examples to read and download.

Summary - **The Presenter**

To reduce the sensation of tiredness in the room, **keep the light on.** To increase attention **blank your PowerPoint when you start.** Also remember to **blank your PowerPoint when you want attention.** Blanking your PowerPoint is easiest done if you get a **remote control.** The remote control gives you the freedom of moving around, **expressing your body language** and making it clear that **you are the presentation. Avoid using the laser pointer,** as it will unnecessarily reduce your body language. Keep **eye contact with the audience** 99% of the time and remember, you can use alternate visual aids. Finally if you want to be a real professional, **introduce the next slide before you show it,** that will make the context clearer to the audience.

Summary - **The Design**

Humans have a weakness in their focus,
therefore keep the focus to
one message per slide.
When designing a PowerPoint slide, strive to
limit your objects per slide to six.
Don't be afraid of having to many slides,
to many slides has never been the problem.
Having long chunks of text is usually
a bad idea if you intend to talk at the same time.
**Don't let the audience read
and listen at the same time.**
Use images instead of or to complement text.
Images are far more efficient
in creating memories. Using animations can be really
good, but take it easy with them,
Only use functional animations.
Another option for creating focus is doing
some magic with
contrast, size and colour
to steer the audience attention.

If you grew with this book

If you felt inspired and grew with this book -
keep an eye open for the next book in the 100-page series:
Presentation Skills - *"It's a skill, not a talent"*

In a unique way this book combines the latest research in the fields of neurology, cognition, psychology and communication with the classic teachings on rhetoric. It's by building presentations that attract the brains of the audience that you, with pure skill, can become a great or even greater presenter and get what you want in life.

The book is very similar in its layout to this book and will of course only encompass 100 pages of examples and straightforward techniques.